MADE IN
TAIWAN

MADE IN TAIWAN

T.C. BROWN

proving
press

Book Design & Production:
Columbus Publishing Lab
www.ColumbusPublishingLab.com

Copyright © 2025 by
T.C Brown
LCCN: 2025911289

All rights reserved.
This book, or parts thereof, may not be
reproduced in any form without permission.

Paperback ISBN: 978-1-63337-942-8
E-Book ISBN: 978-1-63337-943-5

Printed in the United States of America
1 3 5 7 9 10 8 6 4 2

FRONT COVER: Me flaunting some of that Town Patrol swagger, waiting at the Hostel for a ride to work.

BACK COVER: (Left to Right) – Troops cutting loose to the Americanized rock and funk of a Vietnamese band at Bien Hoa, Vietnam.

Partner in crime and in fighting crime, Ulysses Bryant and I pose outside of TAFP's HQ in the Navy Compound in Taichung.

One section of my everyday workplace and American servicemen's playground – The Dirty Dozen.

"What we hunger for perhaps more than anything else is to be known in our full humanness, and yet that is often just what we also fear more than anything else. It is important to tell at least from time to time the secret of who we truly and fully are . . ."

– Frederick Buechner

TO MY MATE, main squeeze and bright shining light Mary Yost, who lifted me up through this drawn-out writing process as I pawed through the younger years of my existence. Heartfelt thanks Mary for improving, with ever-good humor, my slip ups, fumbles and story. Our dreams came true when we found each other late in life, yet your body and spirit left me too soon. Nonetheless, "you" continue to light my way.

This work is also dedicated to my twin daughters, Kelly and Mackenzie, who both vow to read it one day. I started this for you girls so you might one day understand why your dad can be a little goofy and off at times. You both have been two of my greatest blessings and joy in life and I love you both very much. May your lives be filled with passion and adventure.

CONTENTS

INTRODUCTION		i
1.	BETRAYAL	1
2.	WAKE UP CALL	7
3.	BALLS OF BLUE	15
4.	FLYING FOOD	23
5.	UNSOILED	31
6.	GOODBYE COLUMBUS	39
7.	THE DOZEN	45
8.	HUMPING DAY AND NIGHT	53
9.	TAKING CARE OF BUSINESS	61
10.	DROPPING DRAWERS, LOSING FACE	71
11.	TYPHOONS AND TRAINS	79
12.	IN FOR A PENNY	89
13.	DEATH DECISIONS	101
14.	BIEN HOA BLUES	107
15.	TYPING AND TESTING FATE	115
16.	REMF NO LONGER	127
17.	GETTING BOMBED PART II	133
18.	TERRIBLE TUMBLES	141
19.	REVENGE, THE BITTER FRUIT	149
20.	NO BULLETS, NO PEACE	153
21.	DOPES ON DOPE	163
22.	BACK TO THE DOZEN	169
23.	SOARING SENTINELS AND BAR BEEFS	175
24.	PARTNERS, CLOWNS AND BETEL JUICE	185
25.	SMUGGLING STICKS	197
EPILOGUE		209
PHOTOS		217
ACKNOWLEDGEMENTS		233
ABOUT THE AUTHOR		235

INTRODUCTION

AT THE PRIME AGE of 18 at the height of the Vietnam War, I was a naïve, sensitive, semi-virtuous midwestern boy who believed Columbus, Ohio, was pretty much like every other place in the world. Of course, I had not *seen* most of that world.

That innocent but ignorant perspective changed quickly once I enlisted in the Air Force. I rapidly learned I didn't know squat. And then, like it did with everyone else, the military opened its own special brand of whoop ass on me over a period of the first four months.

Those pragmatic shocks to my system were just the beginning of a long and tortuous journey into manhood. The Air Force turned this shy, insecure, devout boy into a baton-wielding cop and then shipped him thousands of miles away from home to Taiwan and later to Vietnam.

For the next five years, I lived in a foreign culture completely alien to me, seasoned by craziness, close friendships, love, violence, reprisals, rampant alcohol and drug use, racial enmity, fierce weather and war.

I was 18 when I left, 23 when I returned home. Those five years had, as we used to say back then, blown my mind. I had witnessed and participated in actions previously never imagined. I had discovered elements of my own personality—some good and some disturbing that pushed the boundaries of my early deep-seated faith—that both pleased and shocked me.

In short, I no longer resembled that teenage wide-eyed innocent. I had gone from straight laced to Crazy Eights. Those times felt like a whole other life. What follows is my best and honest recollection of that implausible rite of passage for a stranger in a strange land during the explosive and turbulent era of the late 1960s and early 1970s. And in a nod to my cradle Catholic upbringing, it's part confessional, too.

Some of it was fun; at times it was scary, a lot of it was crazy, and frankly, more than a little bit of it was seriously illegal. While the following is true, this narrative is not an endorsement for any of the activities I saw or took part in. In fact, I'd encourage you to learn from my mistakes and not make the same bad choices I did.

For years when I told friends anecdotes about my time in Asia, they were fascinated enough to encourage me to write about it. I didn't disagree but I would get bogged down with genre and format as I would begin in fits and starts before shelving the idea. It took decades, but finally it hit me: just write a memoir. And so I have.

I reconstructed this account from documents, memory, mementos, and input from friends and past partners who I managed to track down. Reconnecting with former close friends and working partners from a half century ago was challenging, exciting and even a little intimidating. I was unsure how I'd be received, or even remembered. Would they still like me? And I wondered if it was possible to pick up where we left off from a different life. Turned out, my only disappointment was finding out that a few close associates, including one of my mentors, had died. Those

INTRODUCTION

discoveries made me wish I had begun this journey years earlier. Memories are tricky but I tried to recreate them honestly and I did my best to reproduce events as they actually happened. Some names have been changed to provide cover. I'll let those folks decide for themselves if they want to share their own experiences of those incredible days and nights.

Oh, to go back. When I was writing this memoir, I would listen to the rock 'n' roll and rhythm-and-blues hits from the era. Music from back home played such a critically important role for many of us in those days. Linking the music with memories reignited long dormant emotions, catapulting me back to relive some of the most exceptional and identity-forming experiences of my life. My hope is that you, the reader, especially veterans who sacrificed much to serve our nation, might identify with this tale and find it both engaging and meaningful, too, at least in some small ways.

1
BETRAYAL

HERE I WAS, standing in front of a locked door in Taichung, Taiwan, scared, apprehensive, confused and with my instincts screaming the warning "this is a bad idea!" I feared the worst for what might lay behind that door, literally and figuratively. I swayed side-to-side as I screwed up courage to take action. But what action?

A few shots of whiskey and several beers fueled the journey that put me here in the first place. I was outside of Penny's apartment—my Chinese fiancée. I didn't know for sure if she was cheating on me. But a friend had seen her in the company of another American guy on several occasions. He shared the gut-wrenching news. It was a stunning, heavyweight blow. I didn't want to believe his words, but I had to know for myself.

From 1968 until 1970, I lived and worked in Taiwan as a member of the U.S. Air Force. I had volunteered to go to Vietnam and I was sent there at the beginning of 1970. Now it was mid-November 1970 and I was back. I had returned unscathed from the war but now wondered if I was about to be severely wounded psychologically.

I fell hard for Penny several months after I first arrived in Taiwan in August 1968. She was fun, pretty, accommodating and treated me with some deference, a cultural trait and how many

Asian women treated their men. Six months after we met, I nervously penned a letter to my mom and dad to tell them I wanted to marry her by the end of 1969. Talk about unforeseen and astonishing news from afar.

But instead of getting married, I volunteered to go to the combat zone that was Vietnam. It was the plan I hatched to give Penny and me more time to save money and prepare for marriage and a life in the United States. Bringing a young Asian woman back to America was a complicated and expensive process and it was a heck of a lot to contemplate.

Afterall, we were still kids—I had just turned 20; she was a 19-year-old who would have to move across the globe and live in a country that was foreign to her. But I had correctly calculated that by volunteering for Vietnam, it would be easier for the Air Force to simply re-station me at CCK Air Base in Taichung after my tour of duty because it was relatively close. That way, we could postpone the wedding until I got back, giving us time to get our financial act together and work on cultural adjustments.

I had revisited the island in September on R&R from Vietnam, so it had only been two months since I'd last seen her. It was passionate young love and wrapping my arms around her again was all I wanted to do, and that's about all we did during that too-short of a holiday from war. If there were warning signs of disaster ahead, love blinded me on that visit.

I had promised her I would return and I had thrown myself into the epicenter of danger to honor that pledge. I wanted us to be married. I fervently believed she did too. But then my friend dropped that nightmarish bomb: she might be seeing another man.

BETRAYAL

So here I was, sometime after midnight, in front of that sealed door. I had to find out what it masked. I closed my right fist and banged loudly, shouting out.

"Penny, open the door."

Unsteadily I leaned in and put my ear against the wood. Did I hear whispers? I balled up my right hand again and raised it over my head. Bam, bam, bam, bam, bam!

"Penny, open this door. I know you're in there."

No response. I stepped back, cocked back my right leg and began alternately kicking the door and hammering it crazily with both of my closed fists.

She yelled from the other side.

"TC, stop, wait. I coming."

I stepped back.

She yanked the door open and looked at me and then down to the floor. She stood before me in a barely-closed silk robe, hanging onto the door frame with her right hand and clutching the robe with her left.

I took two steps into the room. Everything I saw in the apartment was little more than an ill-defined blur except for one area. There, as if under a spotlight, was a bed with a half-naked guy on it.

The American was about my age with brown curly hair. He was scrunched back up to the bed's headboard, reaching for his pants laying at the side of the bed on the floor. He was wearing only boxer shorts.

The trauma of this horrifying scene ripped my breath away. I bent over double, hands on my knees as a searing pain cleaved my gut. I was trying to, but could not, disconnect from the repulsive reality assaulting my senses. Instead, a bottomless ache paralyzed me.

Whatever words I said, if I uttered any, have long since disappeared into the mists of time. I remember erupting with tears and emotion. More than likely I said something like "I can't believe this. What are you doing? How could you do this to me? To us? I love you!"

Perhaps Penny had excuses or rationalizations, but the immediate grief closed my ears as my eyes measured the truth. I have no recall of this guy—this cuckold—saying anything at all. Maybe he said, "take it easy," I don't know. I do know I didn't stay long in the room. I turned and ran away from that distressing scene as quickly as possible, as if to make it disappear forever.

At that moment, everything seemed lost. Everything. The real trouble would come later. I didn't know then how deeply this duplicity would impact my life. It changed everything. My experience with a female partner had been limited up to this point and this betrayal colored my relationships with women for years to come.

I lost faith in my ability to trust, which as you will see later, was also hypocritical. I erected soaring defensive walls for protection. I grew leery of commitment. I became more of a glass-half-empty kind of guy who had trouble embracing the calming balm of optimism and hope.

The rage set in soon after this horrific encounter. It was only many years later that I connected the searing pain of this episode—replayed in my head countless times—with the anger that had long rooted itself within my psyche.

BETRAYAL

"Why are you so angry," people have asked over those years.

It puzzled me at times, too. My loss of Penny might not be totally responsible for a deep-seated ire. But I instinctively know that seeing my fiancée in the arms of another so soon after I returned from the war struck a heavy blow to my soul. It also pushed me over a moral line into territory unfamiliar to me—taking revenge on the guy who stole my woman.

Adding cruelty to this foul-tasting and noxious brew of emotions was the momentous decision I had made just prior to my return to Taiwan. A week before I left Vietnam, I had reenlisted in the Air Force to guarantee a return trip to the island.

My reenlistment meant that instead of getting out of the Air Force to return to civilian life in a little over a year, I now would be required to serve an additional four years in the military. Four more years! Are you kidding me?

Oh yeah, I was low down and lost, too.

2
WAKE UP CALL

IN MANY WAYS I was lost from the time I first landed in Taiwan on Aug. 10, 1968. Disbelief at my surroundings provoked that bewilderment, too. As I looked around, my senses immediately took in peculiar sights, sounds and smells that up to then had been inconceivable. I thought I knew pretty much everything about anything and there wasn't a lot that could blow me away. Boy was I wrong.

After we landed at Songshan International Airport in the capital city of Taipei at the north end of the island, an Air Force sergeant directed us to a bus. We muscled overstuffed duffle bags underneath the vehicle and motored a little more than 100 miles southbound, a trip of several hours. Destination: Ching Chuan Kang Air Base—CCK to most everyone—located near the city of Taichung near the west coast and north of the island's center.

I was an 18-year-old kid who was far from worldly but who was certainly naïve. In my mind I had assumed that most places were not all that much different than Columbus, Ohio, my hometown.

I wasn't alone in these unsophisticated beliefs. As our bus traveled the countryside headed to CCK, we ogled countless eye-popping scenes outside the windows and we inhaled an abundance of pervasive exotic and repulsive odors. These new-to-us panoramas thrust most everyone on the bus into culture shock. We were all Alices from America tumbling down an Asian rabbit hole.

We were glued to the windows as endless streams of people on scooters, bicycles, pedicabs and on foot maneuvered madly in and around bumper-to-bumper, wheezing, smoke-billowing buses, speeding taxis and careening cars. All of them competed for space with the occasional slow-moving ox carts on the clogged streets of Taipei.

As we drove on, fires kicked up small plumes of curling smoke everywhere I looked, assaulting our noses with pungent odors of charcoal, burning garbage and, what was that smell, human waste?

Taipei's modern buildings of several stories were topped mostly with Chinese characters intermingled with a smattering of English language advertising. It was all extraordinarily alien to us, but the real double take was the rows of crumbling shanties with uneven corrugated metal roofing. Jammed one next to another, many hung precariously over deep, gigantic gashes in the ground, supported by a mixture of unsteady-looking wooden struts and stone posts.

Clothes hung randomly over lines between bamboo poles, rippling lightly in the breeze, drying in the hot sun in front of or behind many of these hovels. The sizable channels in the ground over which some of the houses hung were called benjo ditches. Dimpled concrete lined the ditches and stretched up 20-25-feet on some banks of the deep troughs.

We quickly learned these canals, necessary in a country prone to unbelievably heavy monsoon rains, also served as open sewers. The "bathroom" in many of these shacks was little more than a hole in the floor. People dumped their waste in the ditches, while others used benjo water to wash themselves or their clothing. Seeing one person brushing their teeth downstream from someone else relieving himself upstream never failed to elicit a "holy shit" reaction, jokes and an "ick" feeling from most of us. If we needed a visceral prompt to not drink the local water, this was it. As we rolled into the flat, gently rolling plains of the landscape we watched farmers in light golden-colored, conical bamboo sun hats, known as Coolie Hats, steering simple wooden plows pulled by long-horned, brown water buffalo slogging through muddy rice fields.

Some people, both in the city and the countryside, shouldered long poles of wood or bamboo with large, heavy-looking pails attached at either end. We had no idea what they were toting and we chose not to think too much about what those buckets might actually hold, either.

In the villages outside Taipei, people milled around small carts that sold street food along the roadside. Bamboo hat-wearing women and men squatted behind their wares either in carts or arranged on makeshift mats right on the pavement. They were hawking vegetables and fruit and flower basket arrangements, or they were wrapping whole fish in string and weighing onions on a long pole "scale" for customers.

We eventually discovered these "noodle stands" stocked many local delicacies. Delicacies for the locals, perhaps, but for me and the other guys it was food from another world.

The stands had cuisine that might include chicken feet, dumplings, steamed buns, animal intestines, notably odd-looking hard-boiled eggs surrounded by a jelly-like casing, duck tongue, blood rice cakes, stinky tofu and—winner of the weirdest food I ever saw someone eat—spicy tiger frog soup. In this strange broth, small half palm-sized, gutted tadpoles literally floated lazily around the bowl.

Yeah, I was a long way from Columbus, Ohio, and not just in ways measured by miles.

Not that mileage was insignificant. My journey of nearly 7,700 miles to Taipei from Columbus, Ohio, began on the chilly 48-degree early morning of March 27, 1968, when I raised my right hand to enlist in the Air Force. With my palm raised, I pledged to "support and defend the Constitution of the United States against all enemies, foreign and domestic."

The oath required a few more standard promises of obedience and service, and by that point my mind was reeling with curiosity, excitement and "what-the-hell-am-I-doing-here" dread. I have no idea why they start this enlistment thing so damn early in the morning.

After the pledge, we sat around for hours with nothing to do. Welcome to the military—it was our first lesson in "hurry up and wait," the standard operating procedure for the armed forces. Many lessons lie ahead, not all good, and we would soon learn one relevant acronym for situations we would encounter in the military: FUBAR—fucked up beyond all repair.

Earlier, my mother, Mary, had roused me from a fitful sleep before dawn. She had prepared breakfast, most likely some combination of eggs, bacon and toast. My grandmother, Tillie, who lived with us, and my 11-year-old brother, Chris, had joined my father, Ed, dressed in his emblematic white shirt and tie, at the table.

WAKE UP CALL

After all these decades our actual words are lost to time. But this last-meal exchange had to be subdued, shaded with sadness and maybe seasoned with some false bravado on everyone's part, especially me.

Eyes welling and gut fluttering, I choked back tears and probably made a lame joke as I said goodbye to my family. The shock that I was actually doing this was starting to set in. My dad loaded my bag into the car and we drove toward downtown Columbus to the Armed Forces Examining Center at Fort Hayes, a military base built during the Civil War.

Once out of the car, my father shook my hand and hugged me. Again I struggled to hold back tears. Being of that era, my dad was not a man who regularly expressed his love in words, and he and I had a strained relationship by now. A few years later, after he died suddenly, my mother told me that when he returned home that day he broke down and cried, a deep-from-the-heart sentiment that clearly revealed his profound love for me.

Calling that day long does not do justice. We were a pack of fresh-faced boyish recruits waiting anxiously in a rickety Fort Hayes building on the verge of a life-changing adventure. Guys dozed, milled about and inspected the clock constantly as time leisurely ticked away, seemingly taking forever to move a minute. I mostly stayed inside my own head, thinking we would get moving at any moment. Why did we have to get here so early? By mid-afternoon, we finally climbed aboard a bus, bound for Port Columbus International Airport.

Hours later and already worn out, we traipsed onto a chartered civilian aircraft that arched into the western skies. We were headed to Amarillo Air Force Base in the middle of the Texas Panhandle in the northernmost area of the state.

By the time we stopped at the Dallas-Fort Worth Airport, made our way to the Lubbock Municipal Airfield, and finally touched down in Amarillo, it was closing in on midnight. We unloaded, boarded a blue Air Force bus and pulled up in front of a building at the air base.

A stocky, stern sergeant in sharply-creased fatigues and a Smokey-the-Bear hat cocked over his brow leapt up the bus steps and stalked the first half of the aisle.

"You boys will unass this bus right now, grab your gear and form a straight line outside!" S.Sgt. Joe Prokop bellowed.

Like proverbial deer frozen in the headlights, we stared, dumbfounded.

"Hey maggots, are you deaf? What the hell are you waiting for? Move your asses! Now!"

As if the seats suddenly discharged blistering heat, we jumped and scrambled into the aisleway, leapt down the steps and grabbed our bags that had already been tossed from the cargo hold of the bus onto the pavement. We did our best to clamber into straight lines in the frosty morning air, made more challenging as the formidable Bus Sergeant and two of his equally bad-tempered, Smokey-the-Bear-hat-wearing comrades, known as TIs or Training Instructors, got right up in our faces and ears, thundering loudly.

If they were aiming to cower us, they succeeded marvelously, at least for me. They herded us into a formation and marched-walked us into a building and into a line serving grease-based eggs, pancakes, toast, bacon and sausage. I think even the juice was part grease. We had 30 minutes to get our food and scarf down what we could.

After the early morning grub they moved us to a large warehouse-size building lined with counters. It was not a pleasant stroll to get there. For TIs, the only way to connect with new recruits was to constantly shout orders, obscenities and insults. These guys were master screechers and I had never heard some of the words they bellowed. And the ones I had heard before had never been used that way around me.

Once inside, we moved slowly forward as the guys behind the counters demanded our shoe and clothing sizes. They tossed large olive-green duffle bags at us that we then stuffed with blankets, sheets, pillows and cases and pairs of fatigues, black boots and hats. The TIs then moved us out and insult-marched us to one of four, two-story barracks squared around an open area known as the quad.

"Walters, get in step! You look like a monkey fucking a football," they shouted at one poor shambling recruit. Unfortunately for him, this poor uncoordinated guy was the tallest of the lot and drew the attention and ire of TIs like a magnet draws filings because he literally stood out. For sure, you never wanted to stick out in any way, shape or form in bootcamp training. Like many of the lessons in my life, I eventually learned this one the hard way.

By the time we were assigned a bunk, made our beds and crawled under the covers, my watch said it was around 2 a.m.

"Hey, boys, it's late so we're gonna cut you a break and let you sleep in a little tomorrow," Prokop promised.

Hmmm, maybe this wasn't going to be so bad after all.

That thought alone confirms my naïveté then. About three hours later, Prokop startled us all when he flipped the lights on and walked down the row of bunks, banging the sides with a nightstick and growling: "Alright dipshits, drop your cocks and grab your socks. Mama ain't here to wipe your noses or your asses no more. You've got 15 minutes to get dressed, make your bed and fall out in the quad! Move it!"

My entire system roiled right into incredulity.

"What have I done? I wanna go home and get back in my bed," I thought, fantasizing that by pulling the covers over my head I could make this horrifying nightmare disappear.

I still didn't understand the "fun" had only just begun.

3
BALLS OF BLUE

OVER THE NEXT six weeks, I had plenty of time to contemplate and regret the gigantic pile of shit I had dropped myself into. Air Force basic training was only the beginning of the hard-knock schooling that would take place over the next few years. That education over time completely transformed who I was.

Growing up in Columbus, Ohio, I was the personification of a fresh-faced, clean-cut lad. Mary, my mother, and Ed, my father, were white and traditional middle-class Catholics. My brother, Chris, was seven years younger, a considerable age gap, and my maternal grandmother, Tillie, had been living with us since I was a youngster and I revered her, likely because she spoiled the hell out of me.

I was a sensitive but happy-go-lucky kid with a taste for music and singing that's stuck with me through the years. As a preschooler, I used to wake my parents from my bed in the morning, serenading them with lyrics from the song "Side by Side."

"Oh, we ain't got a barrel of money, we may be ragged and funny, but we'll travel along, singing our song, side by side."

It was a favorite, perhaps because I sensed or heard my parents talk often about financial difficulties. Guess it was my childish way of trying to ensure the family held things together. Like most kids, I harbored a deep fear of being abandoned. Once around 7-or-8-years-old, I came home from a neighbor's to a locked house, no parent in sight. I went into shock and shed more than a few tears until they rolled up from the store. Fear took hold early in life for me. I avidly consumed books and loved going to the library, but I also absolutely relished television, which in those days was still in its infancy. I would move up and sit so close to the screen I could have been in the show, which probably was the point. I spent a lot of time in front of the tube and sitting on top of it likely fried my eyeballs, which led to glasses by the time I was 12-years-old.

I loved westerns and still remember the scenes where Native Americans overindulged in "fire water" and then began acting crazy. I had no idea at the time these episodes were a precursor for some of my own future adult behavior. The programs were providing a valuable lesson that I failed to heed later in life.

One of my favorite shows was the never-grow-old fantasy of the live TV production of *Peter Pan*. He could fly and the guy never aged! I longed for both. Like almost everyone, I could and often did fly in my dreams. But I embraced the make believe of forever being young without ever really comprehending that I had adapted such a mindset. I'm pretty sure that deeply implanted desire drove a lot of the crazy that I also welcomed later in life.

The Wizard of Oz was another treasured show for me in those days, broadcast annually.

"Somewhere, over the rainbow, bluebirds fly. And the dream that you dare to, oh why oh why can't I?"

I loved that song and the reaching for the rainbow part. But it occurred to me that the development and roots for my own insecurities stem from my inability to obtain some of those dreams, both a subtle and subliminal message, especially during my teen and early adult years. My father was a strict disciplinarian who believed in corporal punishment when he decided I was out of line. I managed to cross those boundaries often enough. He threatened the belt more than once, but most often resorted to applying hand to butt. My dad had a difficult childhood, losing his mother, a sister and a brother while he was still a child.

I wonder now if he too always carried a fear of family loss with him. Why wouldn't he? But like many men of that era, he was not the kind of guy to say out loud that he loved you. I don't remember him saying those words much, if at all. Nonetheless, I instinctively knew it and he did show it at times.

Like the occasion when a bully knocked books out of my hand at the top of a long flight of steps at the library, unaware my father was in a car in the street below. Almost before the books hit the steps, Dad was right there grabbing my tormentor up by the collar and, let's say, strongly suggesting he apologize.

He also taught me valuable lessons that lasted a lifetime. At around 12-years-old I hounded him to let me take drum lessons. He finally agreed, with stipulations. I had to get a job—newspaper delivery, my beginning experience in what later became my career field—and I had to practice a half hour a day, five days a week.

Once I started I could not quit. He intuitively understood my propensity, which still exists, to be easily distracted from objectives by shiny objects that lure me in another direction. Sure enough after about six months I wanted to call it quits, but nope, that wasn't going to happen.

One major lesson drilled into my head by both parents was to not "be a bother to people." That instruction became another foundational operating principle and it wasn't a good fit for my future Air Force career. But it was a code for living and it laid the groundwork for me as a kid, on a pretty regular basis, to fade into the background around a crowd, even on the playground.

As a shy, insecure kid with little confidence, I spent a lot of time living in my own head. It would be noticed.

An eagle-eyed nun would amble over as I leaned against the L-shaped corner of Immaculate Conception elementary school in Columbus. With my head down, I would scrape a foot back and forth aimlessly in front of me.

I was on the playground physically but not mentally or spiritually. As the other kids ran around, chasing and yelling at one another, I was happily somewhere else, in dreamland. Maybe flying or looking for the other side of that rainbow.

"Are you OK?" the nun would ask.

I would look up and smile. "Uh-huh."

"Well, you should go play with the other children. Now go on."

Reluctantly I'd join the squirming mess of kids, but I did little more than wander around. I just wasn't comfortable fully engaging in their play.

As I mentioned, early on I constantly read books or watched TV, which didn't contribute to my athleticism. I was a small, soft kid with glasses, thick lower lip, dark brown hair and flat feet that required me to wear ugly, boxy, brown orthopedic shoes.

I didn't care about sports and I did my best to avoid the challenging confrontations and fist fights common in a youngster's world. I didn't walk around in fear constantly, but the bravery I could muster lived mostly in my mind. I liked to romanticize that

BALLS OF BLUE

I was Spiderman taking down the bad guys. In reality, I was more like Shyman, comfortable hanging out in my personal cocoon.

For the fun of it, a neighborhood kid named Pat McCormack kicked my ass on a regular basis for a while. He'd take me down and pin me to the ground, pounding away. I took these beatings much longer than I should have. One day my dam of anger burst. An electrical charge of rage surged through me. I threw him off, climbed aboard and began to pummel him with clenched fists.

"Terry, Terry, stop! Get off of him," screamed my mother, who had seen us out the side door of our house and run over.

She pulled me off and a stunned and bloody Pat McCormack got off the ground and ran home. He left me alone thereafter. I was as stunned by my eruption as my mother. That was the single major skirmish of my childhood. I didn't know it then, but that was only the beginning for many more to come.

Fear running loose in a young life can lead to dumb decisions that in turn reinforce continued awkwardness. I had no acumen in second grade but I sure proved the wisdom of that truism of fear. As I sat in class one day, what I thought was simply a normal belly rumbling that might be quietly relieved, unexpectedly turned out to be much worse.

I froze. I was panicked and petrified. What to do? Way too soon every kid in the vicinity was making faces and looking around at those near them. They knew something was up. Eventually, so did the teacher.

"Does anyone need to use the bathroom?" she asked.

Wholly frightened and embarrassed, I slowly raised my hand and lowered my head. She kindly led me to the bathroom. In a clear case of blacking out disturbing episodes of life, that's the extent of my memory. No doubt smirks and giggles greeted my entrance back into the classroom. Public shame and fear had now overwhelmingly established a firm and early foothold on my psyche.

Growing up, I didn't drink. I didn't smoke. I didn't cuss. Well, there were a couple of exceptions. When I was about six and at a large family dinner gathering of cousins, I totally mortified my parents when I blurted out during a quiet moment: "I don't like this goddam soup." Mom and Dad expressed shock that I knew such language, but while I didn't hear that around the house constantly, it wasn't totally unfamiliar to me.

And on an outing with a couple of other seniors in high school, showing an early proclivity for wanting to entertain, I got rip-roaring drunk on 3.2 beer by sucking down a couple of enormous glasses through a straw. Brilliant! I was so sick the next day and I couldn't even smell a beer for several years without wanting to vomit.

I faithfully trooped to Catholic Mass and took Communion every Sunday and on holy days. I confessed my "sins" to a priest every month. Hell, I seriously considered entering the priesthood prior to enlisting in the Air Force. Ultimately, I decided I was too intrigued by the opposite sex to cut myself off from any further education in that arena.

If there was even any hint of a crazy streak at the time, it was drumming for The Verdicts, a high school rock 'n' roll garage band. Joining that group was a reaching-the-pinnacle moment for a glasses-wearing nerd like me. But I didn't go wild. I didn't drink alcohol or smoke marijuana. If weed was around, it was an underground activity pursued by others.

Only belatedly did I come to believe that a couple of my bandmates may have clandestinely smoked pot, but I never saw it happen. Even they must have believed that vice was way out-of-bounds for this virtuous teenager. Frankly, the idea of ingesting drugs scared the shit out of me—that is until I turned 21.

Girls scared the crap out of me, too. I usually lost my ability to speak in the presence of a female. In the hierarchy of attractiveness, I believed I resided with the hoi polloi, not the nobility. I just couldn't see why any young lady would like me, let alone love me. Any crush I had on a girl—and there were a couple—developed into a relationship that was carried on, like many things in my life, exclusively in my head. In junior high, during a brief period when we lived in Marion, Ohio, I had it bad for a schoolmate named Sherry. It was 1962, the same year the Four Seasons released their No. 1 hit song "Sherry," which only heightened my "love" for her. I wore that record out, trying to build confidence to approach her and confess my passion.

At the few parties I went to that she attended, I was little more than a wall fixture, observant but soundless. I stalked her neighborhood on a regular basis for a while, walking slowly by her house, first one way, then the other, on the opposite side of the street. Every time I hoped she'd look outside, see me, and emerge to excitedly call me over.

That was my dream and my only real strategy. She never came out but no one called the police either, so there's that. Eventually my family moved and that "relationship" was over.

I finally acquired enough courage to ask out a girl named Rebecca in my sophomore year at Brookhaven High School in north Columbus. We were in a school band together, hung out with a small group of other kids, and soon we were going steady. We became inseparable to the point of dressing alike in matching, brown flowery shirts. It really was a thing in those days.

Nonetheless, in two-and-a-half years I never got much beyond first base. Not that I didn't try occasionally. I was a "good boy," but I wasn't a saint. In the back of my mind I knew there was always Catholic confession, scary as that was.

Sitting in my parent's dark car, we'd start slowly, taking our time and escalating the kisses with wrestling tongues. Then my hands would begin to roam north and south. But as a good girl determined to wait for marriage, Rebecca was unyielding and clamped my wandering paws before I could get to the gold.

I quickly learned that "blue balls" is a real thing—a real painful thing, at that.

4
FLYING FOOD

NOW I'D EXCHANGED blue balls for the blue of the Air Force's uniform. There was plenty of pain involved there, too. I'd swapped my midwestern, idyllic easy life for a realm populated by controlled chaos and always-angry authority figures in Smokey hats bellowing a relentless string of orders and obscenities. I was tossed in with an eclectic mix of guys—white, black, brown, fat, skinny and strapping. They heralded from every corner of the United States, boonies to suburbs to inner city.

But by the end of that first morning in boot camp, only our body size and color distinguished us one from another. The TIs started the day's fun by marching us into a building lined with swivel chairs and leering barbers. Some of them looked gleeful as they held electric clippers, with no attachments.

One after another, we plopped down in the chairs. We offered the cutters a rich field of opportunity. We were all sheep waiting in line to be sheared of our Afros, hair draped to the shoulders or locks hanging just over or above our ears.

Some, anticipating this moment, had shown up to boot camp with short haircuts. Nice try but they couldn't cheat these grim hair reapers who managed to make the trickster's miniscule manes even shorter. It didn't matter what you looked like when you sat, at the end everyone looked pretty much alike. Loud buzzing filled the room. Locks rapidly fell around new recruits' shoulders with every manner and color of curls flying around the room, like a furious wooly blizzard. Some of the barbers smiled widely and joked and whistled as they fervently attacked heads loaded with covering. These were artistes, joyfully at work.

Some recruits appeared on the verge of tears. As clippers buzzed my head, I felt a loss deeper than the one going on up top. Rising out of the chair in the aftermath, I stepped around and through growing piles of hair on the floor. I looked back in the mirror at a stranger.

Dark, wavy curls had been transformed to mere stubble. According to the Air Force, I was now experiencing "team spirit." This rite of passage was designed to make us all equal. At least that's what they told us.

Spirit was something we all needed, desperately. I wasn't the only homesick enlistee, and this was just the first day. Most everyone missed their families and all the comforts home offers. In March 1968, Amarillo was the armpit, or worse and lower in the anatomy, of the Air Force.

The base in the high plains of the Texas Panhandle was activated in 1942. By this time it was literally falling apart. In fact, the Air Force closed and deactivated the base at the end of the year that I was there.

Some buildings had already been abandoned and time and weather had pounded the usefulness out of the ones that housed occupants. Small holes peppered the sheetrock walls in our barracks. It gets frigid in north Texas in March, and when the wind gusts itself into a frenzy and begins to howl, it gains speed over miles of flat-as-a-flattop landscape. It slammed into and shook our barracks and blew dust and dirt through the cracks in the walls, windows and doors on a regular basis. Damn it was cold!

The countryside surrounding the base was so barren and flat, Prokop told us he once climbed a tower and could still see a runaway soldier—Absent Without Leave, or AWOL—a few days after the guy had cut out and booked for the horizon. He was jokingly presenting to us the futility of running away—a court martial offense, by the way—but I know it had to cross some minds.

The first few weeks of basic, especially, were sheer hell and drudgery. They marched us and "double-timed" us everywhere. I drilled for hours in weather that flipped from cold to hot to deluge. And every TI relished getting inches away from our faces, screaming and spraying spittle. What's not to like?

With all the constant and demanding daily physical activity, I shed weight from my chubby frame like a stripper sheds clothes on stage. Facilitating the process were occasional days of 15 or more hours of butt-busting stints of KP—kitchen police duty.

That grind would begin around 4 a.m. and continue mostly nonstop until 8 p.m. I peeled mounds of potatoes, served up gobs of food and washed hundreds if not thousands of dishes and utensils. By the end of a shift, I barely had energy to haul my weary ass up into my top bunk. I fell asleep before my head hit the pillow.

As I mentioned, in boot camp the very last thing you want to do is attract attention or be called out. I had already perfected a disappearing act at teenage parties, so I was well versed in those techniques and did my best to blend into the background. Out of sight, out of mind, hopefully.

But at times, I failed miserably. On one standout occasion I received a hard-earned lesson in physics during lunch. I was the last to arrive with a tray full of food at a small table in the mess hall where three other recruits were already parked.

The large room was packed to the walls with guys, per usual, but the only sound you heard was clinking utensils. Conversation was restricted and we had limited time to finish our meals and fall back outside into formation. As required, I stood in the chow line at attention, empty tray flat against my chest and shuffled along until it was my turn for a server to sling food on a plate and pass it over.

I made my way into the dining area and looked for a spot in the crowded room. Finally I found an empty seat, walked over and set my full tray on the table, pulled out my chair and sat. The tables were small and with three other trays taking up space it was jammed.

As I scooted my chair closer, I rested my forearms on the table and tray's edge. But I had failed to notice something critically important: the near edge of the tray hung over the side of the table.

My arms pushed that edge of the tray down, launching the far end skyward along with all the food on the tray onto my face and chest. As I sat in shock, milk slowly streaming down my glasses, the food, glassware and plates clattered and crashed to the floor. Every head in the mess hall turned to me.

Everyone did their best to stifle what would ordinarily be howls of laughter. TIs emerged from all corners of the room and were on me like hungry bees on a slice of baloney. I was quaking as I struggled to clean up this terrible and terrifying mess.

"What the hell is wrong with you, numb nuts? Don't you know how to sit at a table and eat right?" Prokop roared. "The food goes in your mouth, not on your body, dipshit!

FLYING FOOD

"Clean up this mess, get yourself cleaned up and fall out. Shit! What a dumbass! You're the reason condoms have an expiration date!"

I was the butt of barracks jokes for several days. But I was far from being alone. Humiliation of recruits is one of the main accessories in every TIs bag of tricks. Basic training is designed to break down and remake civilians into soldiers who, without question, will obey orders, including charging headlong into a fiercely fought battle. Instructors apply a succession of stressors each day to challenge recruits both physically and psychologically.

For instance, the TIs seemed to love having middle-of-the-night fire drills. Sure they preached safety but these seemed a little more like harassment. Did we really need to be jolted awake at 2 a.m. on a weekly basis?

Besides the daily degradation and personal insults, the military eliminates privacy, mandates conformity, tightly controls all activities, and pounds recruits with drills that seem to make little, if any, sense. The overarching goal of the Air Force and all branches of the service is to build bonds of mutual loyalty and get everyone to work as a team.

The NCOs—non-commissioned officers—running us were journeymen at breaking us down with preposterous tasks. When one person screwed up, the rest of us usually shared in the consequences. No doubt they found it entertaining.

One of their little schemes and a dreaded form of torture for us was known as the "nose-to-toes" drill. Someone would break a rule and we'd all be lined up on both sides of the barracks hallway, backs to the wall. Then a TI would bark out the order to "about face" so our noses and toes would be crammed up against the wall.

This would go on seemingly forever and our snouts and toenails had better be touching that wall.

One continual headache—and there were many—was ensuring you made your bed drumhead tight. Prokop and the other tormentors had to be able to bounce a quarter off the top blanket and catch it in the air. They tested us constantly. Contrived or not, early on in training a couple of us failed to make our beds to their satisfaction. That's all it took.

Prokop barked at the entire floor.

"You maggots are stupid and useless. After all this time, you still can't make a bed properly. Mommy's not here to hold your hands, boys. You dipshits *will* learn how to make a bed right!

"Rip all of your bedding and mattresses off these bunks right now and hustle them down into the quad. Dump them in a pile and fall the fuck back in!"

For a beat, we all were paralyzed as we tried to digest this insane order.

"Well, what the fuck are you waiting for dummies? Get your asses movin'!"

What a mad scramble that was! We tore off pillows, pillow cases, sheets, blankets and mattresses. We manhandled them downstairs and outside, banging into each other, knocking one another down and then dumping everything onto the ground. We then stood at attention, like a dishonor guard, in front of a gigantic mound of bedding.

"OK, shit-for-brains, here's what you're gonna do. You are going to jump in that pile, grab your bedding and then haul ass back in there and make your damn bed air fucking tight!

"When I come back in 20 minutes, if I can't bounce a quarter off that bed, your problems will have only just begun. Got it? Now move!"

It was on! Every man for himself. Guys were shoving and elbowing and cursing as they struggled to grab the right number of sheets, blankets, pillows, pillow cases and a mattress.

We stumbled and fell or were shoved, elbowed and knocked down as everyone dove in and snatched bedding. Then we had to drag all of that stuff back up into the barracks and back to our bunks.

Fearing the consequences of an angry TI, I dove into the melee and somehow managed to pull out the right amount of bedding. Half falling up the stairs, arms full, I struggled back to my bunk, dragging bedding behind me. Each tick of the clock triggered more drops of sweat.

I made the tightest bed I had ever made in my life. Nonetheless, I was literally shaking with fear as Prokop clomped down the aisle, drawing closer.

When he got to me, he plunged a quarter toward the blanket. Mercifully, it bounced back up. "Good job, buttercup. Make it like this every time, ya hear?"

"Yes, sir," I barked back, eyes straight ahead, back ramrod straight.

I had survived to live another day of fun in Air Force boot camp. Scarier times lie ahead.

5
UNSOILED

THE SUN DESCENDED slowly on a flawless summer Texas day as we lounged on the ground after tromping off a bus at Camp Bullis, several miles from Lackland Air Force Base in San Antonio, Texas. Some of the troops were engaging in the usual amount of joking and grab ass, but myself and a few others were quietly pensive.

The reason? We were about to face a mission way more daunting than making an air-tight bed in boot camp for the stalking TIs at Amarillo. Somehow I had managed to survive and successfully plow through the daily horrors of basic training about five weeks previously.

Afterward, I was sent immediately to Security Police Technical School at Lackland. So here I was in the final week of that training and as the once-blue sky spun into dusk, I mentally prepared to embark on the scariest and toughest assignment I had faced since enlisting.

In this assault exercise, we would begin by belly crawling out of a trench cradling an M2 carbine under barbed wire as M50 machine guns fired live tracer rounds just over our heads. If that didn't get your attention, the explosions that trainers set off in pits surrounded by mounds of dirt that we crawled by would. Yikes!

As if we needed to be reminded, a range instructor laid out the peril.

"Not long ago, one idiot panicked and stood up. With live machine gun rounds flying overhead, not a good idea, people," he said matter of factly. "That boy was cut in half. You know what lesson that teaches?"

We all looked at one another silently.

"Don't stand up, dipshits."

Now I don't know if that instructor's story was true, but it certainly got my attention. Before the mock assault began, I looked eastward at the dusky sky and clung desperately to memories of home, where I would soon be headed if I survived this. It was my way to cope as the minutes ticked by and I drew closer to potential death.

What were my girlfriend and family doing right this minute? I ached to be with them, especially Rebecca, who I just wanted to hold and squeeze tightly. Would I ever get that chance again? What if this was my last night on earth? As the sky changed from blue to hues of orange and red, I was reminded of something. Blood!

Once it was dark enough, someone switched on the field tower lights. Trainers whistled us into formation and into the trenches.

"Hit the dirt and crawl for your lives. And don't stand up, dummies!" the instructors screamed.

Heart racing and cradling my Korean War-vintage rifle, I pushed with my knees and pulled with my forearms as I crawled up a small rise out of the trench. I saw entanglements of barbed wire stretched knee high across the field, from my left to my right.

As I literally tried to burrow into the dirt, I shoved myself toward the first strand of wire and jumped—internally, not up—as the machine guns opened up. "Rat, tat, tat, tat, tat, tat, tat. Rat, tat, tat, tat, tat, tat, tat. Rat, tat, tat, tat, tat, tat, tat." Red tracers every 10th round or so zipped overhead from the strategically placed weapons in bunkers to one side.

I tried to crawl deeper into the packed dirt and rock. I was scared shitless, but only just. I finally inched my way past one of the many small mounds to my left that dotted the field.

"Ka-booooom!" The explosion sent a small shower of dirt pinging off my helmet as I jammed my face into the ground and stopped dead.

"Keep moving, ass wipes!" came the amplified voice from high above in a tower.

I figured he was talking to me but I didn't care, I was ready to stop this irrational show. I had not soiled myself, yet, but I definitely wanted to be done with this madness. It seemed the only way to end the terror was to crawl forward out of the nightmare.

Ears ringing and limbs quivering, I dug deep and continued to drag myself forward under the wires and machine gun fire and past the explosions.

Somehow, I managed to get through to the end with no more than a few scrape marks on my hands and arms. My pants remained dry, too. The feeling afterward was euphoric. That's what winning a reprieve from death will do for you.

Many of the other guys were laughing and talking excitedly. We had all accomplished a serious military mission, even if it only amounted to not getting our heads blown off or soiling our underwear. I had faced real terror and danger and pulled myself through it to the other end.

"I can get through dangerous, crazy, scary stuff."

That thought gave me some hope that I might be a little tougher than I had believed. While I never much contemplated it, the revelation helped get me through more than a couple of traumas and brawls during my time in the military as a cop, especially when facing down drunk, uncooperative guys who'd rather fight than comply.

This unforgettable affair was the capstone of six weeks of sky cop training. One other earlier memorable field drill was what I call "find the hidden sniper without getting killed first."

It resembled today's paintball games, only way ahead of its time and without the paint. As I carefully crept around trees and through the brush, sometimes on hands and knees, I learned quickly and the hard way that it's damn near impossible to find someone camouflaged and hiding in the woods, even if they are intent on killing you. I "died" several times during that afternoon's exercise.

In the Air Force, security police are responsible for law enforcement and security of the flight line and air base. So most of those past five weeks in tech school had been dominated by training in physical drills, defensive maneuvers, practice guarding aircraft replicas—what we called humping—and learning various restraints, take downs and arrest holds and procedures.

My least favorite technique, but highly recommended, was the so-called police arm bar. Someone resisting arrest? No problem. Grab his arm and quickly twist and whip it around behind his back, theoretically incapacitating him. My faith in this tactic was always shaky at best. And rightly so. Over the years more than one strong-arm guy twisted his way out of this hold and tried to clean my clock before I could force his arm up high on his back. I understood the importance of gaining control in such situations, but too many times there was a little voice inside that warned, "Don't hurt this guy."

Probably not the best instinct or impulse for a cop to have.

More than once I believed I was in the wrong profession. I didn't have the demeanor or physique to be a police officer. With a 5-foot 9-1/2-inch, 170-pound frame, chances of me intimidating anyone were slim, at best. Plus, I was kind of a quiet guy, more of a loner than a mixer. Family and friends expressed shock when they learned I would become a cop.

Law enforcement had not been a career-goal desire, either. I joined up thinking I would be able to get in an Air Force band like a couple of my former high school bandmates had done in the Army.

After all, the Air Force recruiter told me, "No problem, just tell them that's what you want to do when you get out of basic training."

Hook and line cast, green, unsophisticated recruit snared. Too late, I discovered it doesn't work that way. In the closing days of basic training, I was told I had three choices—cook, air traffic controller or police. After the KP duty I had recently experienced, being a cook had zero appeal and you needed 20-20 vision to work in a control tower—mine was more like 20-200. Sky cop it was despite my past avoidance of all things related to fighting.

I realized the work likely would send unexpected and dangerous encounters my way and that made me more than a little nervous. Could I do this job well? But it also sparked an awareness that I would have clout over other people. I represented the law and safety.

While it was an immense responsibility, it was also kind of cool to have that authority, which probably helped boost my fondness for being in control of situations, a trait I still kind of like.

Finally on July 5, 1968, I got my wings, so to speak, and graduated from tech school as an airman—the non-flying kind. The Air Force let me go home on leave for one month to regale family, girlfriend and friends with tales of the horrors and daring-do involving live bullets, scrubbing pots and peeling potatoes all-day, running and marching everywhere and TIs who started each day at 5 a.m. by shrieking insults about you and your girl back home, "Suzy Rottencrotch."

That was the great news.

The harsh news? Myself and 11 classmates were ordered to report to McChord Air Force Base in Tacoma, Washington, in early August to board a flight bound thousands of miles from home. We were assigned to the 6217th Security Police Squadron in the 6217th Combat Support Group, located at an airbase in the middle of Taiwan, wherever that was. Turns out the island lies roughly 100 miles off the southeast coast of China, separated by the Taiwan Strait, which is part of the South China Sea. The central mission of the base was to support the U.S. war efforts in Vietnam. We'd be on assignment overseas for 15 months on a tour of duty the Air Force classified as isolated and remote.

Man oh man. Goodbye Columbus and family, friends and girlfriend Rebecca. Through hugs and tears, the girlfriend and I fervently promised to be faithful until my return. Clueless as to what was to come, I would soon learn that pledge would be the first consequential broken assurance in my life, leading to titanic changes.

Without a doubt, the real adventure was about to begin.

6
GOODBYE COLUMBUS

WE HAD BEEN on the bus out of Taipei for more than three hours when we turned away from the coastal highway at the hamlet of Ching Sui to ascend a very narrow, steep road up to the top of a plateau leading to CCK Air Base.

The journey from the states, with a rest stop in Guam, had already been protracted, grueling and harrowing enough. But one peek outside of the window as our careening bus chugged up that steep roadway chased away any lingering cobwebs. I was peering down into the maw from a sheer cliff and my weariness was instantly wiped out. Were we going to survive long enough to reach the base?

Surprisingly, we made it to our destination without sideswiping an ox cart or plowing over the many bicyclists and motorcyclists we blew by. They were everywhere and many were shakily trying to balance a wife or kid or a leaning tower of baskets or other cargo strapped and perched on the back of their vehicles.

After stopping at the main gate and showing IDs to a sharp-looking security policeman in a white hat and khakis walking down the aisle, we motored to a building for a check-in procedure where we got processed, had a short briefing and then were assigned a room in the barracks. Afterward, we were left to our own devices to kick back and explore the base.

CCK was located about 10 miles from Taichung. With a population of around 400,000, it was one of the island's larger cities after the capital Taipei. The island is 235 miles long and about 90 miles across at its widest and is shaped roughly like a tobacco leaf.

The Central Mountain Range, with peaks as high as 13,000 feet, sits east of Taichung. Rolling hills dominate the north, and flat coastal plains stretch across the south and west. Most of the island's population of 11 million lived on those fertile coastal plains. CCK was a Nationalist Chinese military base and the U.S. Air Force was a tenant on about 225 acres of the property.

Taiwan's earliest people were head-hunting tribesmen of Malay, some of whose descendants still lived in the mountains of the east coast when we arrived. Thankfully, by then, they had renounced their love of collecting noggins.

Chinese settlers in the 7th Century called the island "Taiwan," which means "Terraced Bay." Portuguese who landed around 1590 named the island "Liha Formosa," which translates to "Beautiful Island."

Taiwan was ceded to the Japanese in 1895 after they won a three-year war with the Ching Dynasty of China. The Japanese modernized the island and held a tight rein over the population until the Allies defeated them in 1945 in World War II.

In 1949, Taiwan had an indigenous population of about six million people when the Chinese began to leave the mainland in droves and move onto the island. The exodus began after Chiang Kai-shek's Nationalist forces lost control of the mainland following years of civil war with Mao Zedong's Communists.

An estimated two million Chinese fled to the nearby island, where Chiang declared martial law, which was still the law of the land when I arrived. The Nationalists set up a government-in-exile called the Republic of China.

Those beginnings were accompanied by a vicious political repression. Over several decades, Chiang had thousands of locals killed and imprisoned in a period that became known as the White Terror.

Even without all of that background knowledge—it wasn't something discussed or even barely known among most American troops—the friction between native Taiwanese and the Chinese could be detected at times.

For instance, the mainland's mother tongue of Mandarin was predominantly spoken on the island, while the government discouraged use of the Taiwanese language. But our focus was on the mission at hand. The American side of the base provided operational and logistics support to units throughout the western Pacific, especially in Vietnam. The 314th Tactical Airlift Wing conducted those operations with its aircraft, pilots, crews and maintenance people.

And the brass wanted to ensure we all understood that we were guests on this island whose government was "essentially at war with the mainland." The Nationalists fully intended to recapture China someday, even two decades after landing on the island. The CCK welcoming booklet we received also warned that "both overt and covert intelligence activities are carried on constantly" and that we should avoid phone and public discussions of sensitive topics.

The pamphlet also reminded us that "the most important thing that you must bear in mind during your tour at CCK is that we are all guests of the Chinese government . . . and your bearing and conduct have a direct influence on the relationship we enjoy with our hosts."

We were the foreigners here and that was a constant reminder for us Americans, beginning from our very first orientation briefing.

"The Chinese are our hosts and you will act accordingly, with honor," the first sergeant warned. "Don't do anything stupid and bring shame on yourselves or your country."

As we would soon discover, such wise advice did not take hold with everyone, myself included.

Giant hangers defined the CCK flight line, populated by rows of camouflaged, four-prop C-130E cargo aircraft and KC-135 refueling tankers. The KCs are similar to the Boeing 707, but have an extendable flying boom at the tail. The booms can hook into and gas up other aircraft in the air that are flying below the KC. Soon enough, I would get to know these "birds" up close and personal, both in the heat of the day and in icy, inclemently wet nights. I was assigned the job of guarding this multimillion-dollar machinery with my life, no matter what Mother Nature was doing to the weather around me.

The base offered numerous opportunities for recreation. It had a swimming pool, bowling alley, theater and a tape library to record reel-to-reel music, a favorite activity for many of us in those days.

You could attend chapel, eat at a couple different chow halls and throw down cheap Schlitz beer, pickled eggs or free champagne on your birthday at the CCK Airmen's, NCO or Officers' clubs, depending on your rank. The watering holes offered nightly entertainment with Chinese bands and singers like Lulu doing their best to imitate the hits of American rock 'n' roll and soul music stars.

Another hot spot was the MARS (Military Affiliate Radio Station) building, a cinder-block structure where you waited, often in a long line outside, for a turn to call home via a scratchy sounding ham radio.

It was always a bizarre, fumbling experience because you were required to say "over" every time you finished a sentence, followed by a short delay of silence before you would hear Mom, Dad or the girlfriend respond.

"Hi honey, I love you, over." Silence.

"I love you too, over." Silence.

We were each assigned a room with bunk beds in one of the two-story, H-shaped, gray corrugated steel barracks. A bus stop for the "CCK Smoker," so named for its propensity to spew clouds of noxious tailpipe fumes as it motored along, was nearby.

That bus stop became our link to another world—the city of Taichung and its foreign culture and everything it offered. And this ride into a new world cost only 25 cents! The trip offered charms and mysteries unimaginable to me at the time.

In a day, we'd be allowed to go off base at night to explore after our daily briefing. My first venture to town was basically unplanned. But it certainly became the momentous escapade of a lifetime up to that point and one I can still remember decades later.

Many of us were eager to hit the town to check out for ourselves what a whole bunch of guys couldn't wait to tell us about—the Dirty Dozen. While called The Dozen, in reality it was a couple of blocks of more than 12 bars, catering to the American GI with booze, bands and, well, broads.

We'd already had our minds blown by all the new-world-to-us stuff we'd seen on the trip down from Taipei, so we couldn't wait to see up close what all this buzz was about outside of CCK's Main Gate. The gossip of girls galore working in the bars on The Dozen sharpened that anticipation.

The U.S. military was not clueless to these temptations and the perils they presented, of course. And with the prevalence of venereal disease, they made sure we were educated about the denizens of "The Dozen" and their potential to generate medical problems.

"Look fellas, just be careful of the company you keep," a master sergeant jokingly advised during a gathering the next morning. "Most of the girls down there in town either have VD or TB, so if you don't want your pecker to fall off, I'd advise you to find a girl who's coughing."

Sage advice, kind of. In the long run, however, many failed to heed those warnings. When the inevitable occurred, they would then be compelled to line up at the medical clinic for a shot of penicillin.

Infections were so common the hospital handed out round red patches with a white and black cartoon character holding spears and the words "penicillium curare" underneath to be given to the unlucky ones. That medication, no doubt, had to be constantly restocked.

7
THE DOZEN

FINALLY, IT WAS time to head to town. Several of us jumped aboard the Smoker, which turned left after chugging through the Main Gate. The blue bus, with a destination sign that either said "Taichung" or "CCKAFB," depending on the direction it was headed, had an open window at every seat and a permanently closed window just above it.

The vehicle always provided an interesting and sometimes harrowing 30-minute ride into town. A "bus girl" who spoke passable English rode along and helped translate requests from American passengers to the Chinese driver.

We passed fields and rice paddies for the majority of the trip to town, but within 10 minutes or so outside of the Main Gate around a curve, the bus passed a small gathering of bars known as "Bar Town" in a place called Ta Ya Village—translation: "Little Alley"—off of the main highway. Some guys got off here, but the main attraction was still farther up the road.

Shortly thereafter, the bus approached an intersection in town and turned left onto a street named Wu Chuan Lu across from the big Monte Carlo bar where it stopped to let us off. At last, the epicenter of all the action and blather.

I jumped off the bus and looked down the street. Stretching out before me was a raft of bars, one after the other, lining both sides of the roadway. Signs proclaiming their American names, accompanied by outsized Chinese characters to the side or over the top, competed for attention and laughs.

Among the lot were the "Paris Bar," "OK Bar," "US Lounge," "Monte Carlo," "Playboy Bar" complete with rabbit logo, "Top Hat Club" with a large top hat laying over a black cane, "Camel Bar," "Hollywood Club," "Bluebird Tavern," "China Club," "Ruby Club," "Your Snack Bar," "Mustang Club," "Butterfly Club," "Wagon Wheel," and the misspelled "'Clud' Little Woman," all nestled against one another.

There was even a Sheraton Hotel that had large Chinese characters on a roof sign, while underneath in English it said: "BAR. BALL. ROOM."

This midwestern boy from Columbus looked around in awe at this adult Disneyland. Although I'd never been, I imagined this setting to be a little bit like a cheaper version of Las Vegas, with much less glitziness and sparkle and way more oddities. As a few of us wandered down the street together, Chinese guys stood in the doorways of the bars, doing their best to get us to step inside.

"Hey GI, pretty girl inside. Strong drink. Cheap. Veddy cheap."

I smiled shyly, ignored the entreaties and moved on. Some guys couldn't wait and entered the first bar they saw. A couple of us kept walking and sightseeing, and there was so much to witness.

The environment, not unlike a modern-day flea market, washed over all five senses. Chinese people shuffled by in flip flops as vendors squatted behind baskets or carts on the side of the

THE DOZEN

street or yelled at us from shops crowded with food, clothing and other merchandise.

Some were selling pirated American hit record albums for 10 NT$ (New Taiwan dollars) that equaled 25 cents in U.S. money. Other peddlers had eye-catching trinkets, fascinating home decorations and even hibachi stoves made from American beer and soda cans collected and repurposed by creative, savvy Chinese trash pickers. It was our first early experience with recycling!

Some hawked vegetables, fruit, meat and other products we couldn't identify. Several noodle stands, with dried octopus and chicken feet hanging from the top rim of the carts, attracted a brisk business. We also discovered Taichung Mongolian Bar-B-Q, which quickly became a favorite place to eat for many Americans. The restaurant was more stir fry than barbeque, where cooks used extended chop sticks to fry your choice of meat, vegetables and condiments on a hot flat pan. The food was served in a bowl with pita-like bread that could be stuffed with the concoction and you could go back for refills as much as you wanted.

A legacy was born. Years after I returned to the U.S., Mongolian barbecues began to open around the country, including a couple in Columbus. I'm guessing some of the owners came from Taiwan or had first-hand experience with this tasty fare from their time in the military.

Mingled in with the bars and restaurants, laborers in storefronts weaved rattan strips to create furniture, while others carved Chinese mountain and battle scenes into camphor wooden tables, desks or into the backs of chairs.

All of this action was head spinning and the products were dirt cheap. Tailor-made suits, teak and rattan furniture, gorgeous detailed artwork and intricately carved wooden sculptures were hot items. By the end of their service time on the island, most airmen had stocked their rooms with prized purchases, which they then shipped back home, courtesy of the Air Force.

We finally chose a bar to check out. As we entered, several "bar girls" dressed in slit-up-the-thigh mini-skirts descended on us like packs of famished locusts. They had a sixth sense for spotting greenhorns and they chattered away and grabbed for our hands to get our attention.

"Hey GI, long time no see, short time for free."

It was a standing joke for them, but not always, of course. They did keep track of us Americans. After you became friends with a young lady and then failed to stop by for several days or longer you'd hear, "Hey, where you been. You butterfly me."

It was her way of saying you must have been cheating on her with another girl.

Most of the women were pretty and many looked very young. Some stood out, like the lady known as "BB The Machine." To say this woman was well-endowed would be a serious understatement. Stories, true or not, about her "abilities" constantly made the rounds on the base. BB was elevated to near mystical status over time and was one of the first local legends new arrivals would learn about.

Every bar had its own horde of young girls who had one mission—to get you to buy them as many overpriced drinks as possible. Many consumed some kind of pink or red concoction, most likely with zero alcohol content.

Every bar had a manager, aka "mama-san." She was the big boss and the girls always showed her proper respect. You could pay mama-san a fee to take one of the girls out of the bar on a "date." Sometimes it literally was just a date to go out to eat or to go to a club to dance. Some of the women could be more direct: "You want boom-boom?"

It didn't take a Mensa member to understand what that particular slang meant.

Being new, it took us a little time to learn how all these transactions worked. But initially, we were like wide-eyed kids with a raging sweet tooth who just got turned loose on a street packed with ice cream shops with a whole lot of varieties.

That first day we spent hours hopping from bar to bar, blowing money on liquor-less drinks for the chicks and alcohol for ourselves. I still was not a drinker at this point in my life and I still couldn't stand the smell of beer. Over the evening, I experimented with a few sips of plum wine, a popular local beverage, so as a rookie it didn't take much for me to catch a buzz.

The women, the bars, the booze and the pretty much anything-goes ambiance worked its magic on my intense, inexperienced libido. That pledge of faithfulness I promised Rebecca grew fainter and fainter in my memory until it disappeared in a vapor. I was still a virgin, but suddenly a new boldness arose, among other things.

I began to seriously consider that it might be time to surrender my virginity. So, attracted by a barker-like, thin Chinese guy, myself and a buddy ended up in front of a whorehouse on our first night in town.

Now what I knew about lovemaking at this point had all come from books. Sex was like the 8th Wonder of the World for me. The house we entered was dimly lit. We completed a financial transaction and then a dark-haired Chinese woman, looking to be in her early-to-mid 30s, led me to a small, dank, incense-smelling, candle-lit bedroom with a cracker-thin mattress. My buddy was led to a different room by another woman.

Even I could tell this lady was a veteran. I was definitely a nervous apprentice. If there was any conversation, it was minimal, which pretty much matched the amount of time I spent to complete this act of "love." It was over so quickly I was left wondering, "What just happened?"

I lay there for a minute looking at the ceiling with her by my right side. I looked over at her.

"Let's do it again," I suggested nimbly.

In a kind of "say what?" double take, she looked at me like she had just spotted a third eye in the middle of my forehead.

"More boom-boom, you pay again," she replied in a matter-of-fact all-business manner.

I considered the offer but decided I had done enough damage for my first excursion into town. I still had more than a year left here. I got dressed, said goodbye and found my buddy.

By this time, the sky was starting to lighten in the east. The Smoker was not yet running, so we grabbed a taxi and hauled ourselves back to base. By the time we got to the barracks and showered up, we had missed chow. We hustled over to the daily briefing and took seats just as the indoctrination was beginning. More than a few eyebrows were raised.

"Glad you boys could make it," growled the sergeant leading the session.

Thankfully no official role call had occurred and we had not been missed at chow.

THE DOZEN

We surreptitiously hid grins, but a lot of the other guys around us did not. For some, we were already legends with only one day under our belts on the island. Others thought of us as idiots, I'm sure. The latter group was more accurate.

This overnight affair was simply the harbinger of things to come.

8
HUMPING DAY AND NIGHT

THE AIR FORCE changed the name of my career field in 1966, two years before I enlisted, from air police to security police. The service decided the new name was more applicable, concise and descriptive because it combined both elements of the mission—law enforcement and security of air bases. Nonetheless, many folks referred to us in the slang of "sky cops."

As an apprentice airman it was practically guaranteed that for my first job I'd be assigned to guard aircraft on the flight line for eight hours at a time on both day and night shifts. I was. Before each shift I ensured my black boots were spit shined and my green fatigues were ironed with sharp creases. I snapped my silver police badge, topped by an eagle, around the button on my left breast pocket.

A blue name tag, with "Brown" stitched in white, was sewn over the top of my right pocket. Underneath on the pocket itself was a blue, white and gold embroidered "Pacific Air Force" patch. It had an arc across the bottom cradling a globe, capped by a gold wing around the right side and with gold stars, a leaf and a thunderbolt over the sphere. Looking good and sharp was always required.

Before reporting for inspection with the rest of the "flight"—Air Force terminology for a unit of airmen—I checked out an

M-16 from the armory. I wore either a combat helmet while patrolling around the aircraft or a green ball cap if I was scheduled to man one of the traffic entry control points to the flight line.

During regular inspections the bosses were looking for those razor-sharp creases in your fatigue shirts and pants, which were bloused snugly over the top of boots bright enough to reflect lights on the flight line. It took me a while to learn these techniques when I entered boot camp, but by now I had it down. I wiped out boxes of cotton balls rubbing black shoe polish into those boots.

Our work was divided into a nine-day cycle. The first round started with a swing shift beginning at 3 p.m. After three days, we'd be off for 24 hours, but usually had to attend a scheduled training. Then we'd report for three days of work beginning at 11 p.m. Another day off after that round and we'd work three-day shifts. The cycle ended with 72 hours off and then we'd start it all over again.

The schedule was designed to break up the monotony of working the same shift all the time and to help keep us sharp out on the flight line. Whatever the reasons, the continual change in work hours did accomplish one thing—it eliminated any chance of having a normal sleeping schedule.

The days and nights were long and boring. I paced around KC-135s, watched over C-130s and occasionaly patrolled the mind-blowing wing span of gigantic B-52s that dropped in if the bomber had in-flight problems or was avoiding typhoons in other parts of Asia. It was a lonely, grinding job. I counted steps as I moved around to distract myself from tedium.

As much of a slog as it could be, in some ways it was ideal for a loner like me. Daydreaming was a perpetual companion. It was like the old days of hanging around the elementary school playground, only this time with a radio and an assault weapon, guarding millions of dollars of expensive war equipment.

But I had to be careful not to get too lost in reverie. After all, being an alert guard was the point. And the chiefs tested our vigilance on a regular basis. They would try to slip someone through a checkpoint without proper identification in a flight line intrusion exercise. Occasionally, the attempted breach was more in-your-face.

One morning around 3 a.m., I was walking around the front of a KC toward the back of the aircraft when I thought I spotted movement 100 or more yards away, near the taxiway lights.

I quickly unshouldered my M-16 and moved under the wing, closer to the boom at the rear of the aircraft. Inching forward, my hands cradled my rifle as my left thumb rested on the safety above the pistol grip and my right index finger lay outside the trigger guard.

My heart started pounding. I squinted and peered into the dark, attempting to look between the lights. I saw a figure that had been crouching trying to crab walk away in the grass at the edge of the tarmac.

"Halt! Stop right there or I'll fire," I screamed into the night, the butt of the M-16 now nestled into my right shoulder with the barrel pointed directly at him. The dim figure quit moving.

"Stand up slowly and raise both hands over your head!"

A man rose and lifted both of his hands.

"Step forward onto the tarmac."

He did so carefully, both hands still in the air. I could see he was also dressed in fatigues, with no markings.

As I moved a bit closer, I said, "Get down on your knees and lay flat on the ground, with your arms and hands extended above you. Do it now!"

Once the guy was prone, I radioed in that I had detained an intruder. I stood close, but not too close, weapon pointed at the man as I waited for my flight chief to roll up in a jeep.

Turns out the trespasser was a "play actor" from another flight.

"Good job, Brownie," my boss said, patting me on the shoulder.

It wasn't the last test, but whether on the line or at an entry point, no one got by me who wasn't supposed to be there. You never knew when they would pull incursion exercises. They also understood the value of breaks and the boss man would swing by in a jeep a few times over a shift, often with coffee, so I could take the load off for a bit, especially in crappy weather. That was particularly helpful during the long overnight shifts, which, weirdly enough, I did love at times.

It was so cool to look up into the sky on a clear night and see hundreds of stars. I always searched for the three bright ones in a line, which I didn't know at the time but later learned was Orion's belt. They became my own personal North Star for some reason, and I felt comfort in being out there alone and being able to see them. It wasn't always a beautiful outdoor experience roving the flight line. Taiwan's climate is a combination of tropical to subtropical, which meant the summers were hot and could run from April or May all the way into September or October. The climate was comparable to the southern parts of Texas and Louisiana.

With an average rainfall of up to 100 inches per year, monsoons rolled through on a regular basis and when they did, the rain roared out of the sky in solid sheets. One minute you were dry as a desert; the next you were soaked to the bone, even wearing a poncho, and standing in a couple inches of flowing water on the tarmac. Monsoons made it clear why benjo ditches crisscrossed the countryside.

I was excited when I reported for a dayshift on January 2, 1969. Back in Pasadena, California, it was the afternoon of January 1 and the Ohio State football Buckeyes, undefeated and top ranked in the country, were set to take on the University of Southern California Trojans, the No. 2 team, in the Rose Bowl.

The Rose is called "The Granddaddy of Them All," so named as the oldest college football bowl game. And this was only the second time a No. 1 had met a No. 2 in a Rose Bowl matchup. OSU may have been top dog, but the other guys had Heisman Trophy winner O.J. Simpson, infamous much later on for all of the wrong reasons.

It was an historic matchup and I wasn't about to miss it, work or not. I had no choice! Born in Columbus, my parents indoctrinated me into Buckeye Nation the moment I began to understand words.

"We are Buckeyes. We bleed scarlet and gray," they explained, referencing the team colors.

It didn't matter that neither of them went to OSU; every year they bought season tickets for the home games and my mother continued to attend those games for 59 years—into her 80s—until she passed.

So being thousands of miles away from this momentous matchup, I did what any scarlet-and-gray-blooded American would do. I smuggled a transistor radio with white plastic earphones—today known as earbuds—onto my post so I could listen live while I patrolled the line for my country. No doubt my clandestine scheme would have been seriously frowned upon by the chiefs and could have caused me problems. But my main concern at the time was that they might test me with an intrusion exercise during the game. And what a game it was! Good thing it's noisy on a flight line during the day.

"Crap, c'mon Buckeyes," I yelled when Simpson burst through tacklers for an 80-yard touchdown in the second quarter.

Simpson scampered for a solid but scary-for-me 171 yards in the game. But he also fumbled for one of USC's five turnovers. A casual observer may have thought I was swatting away insects at times.

"Yeah, way to go Buckeyes!" I shrieked, pumping my arm across my chest with a closed fist after our strong-armed quarterback Rex Kern threw two touchdown passes in the fourth quarter to seal it.

Final score: OSU 27—USC 16.

Luckily, no one interfered with pesky drills or tried to sneak onto the tarmac. They might have made it in! During my first five months on the island humping airplanes, that day went by the fastest and it was the most fun shift I worked. For the most part, my life was uneventful and pretty much centered around work and training in those early months. After that initial wild excursion when I first arrived at CCK, I only went to town occasionally because I wasn't much of a drinker. I had more than proved my drinking inexperience on my 19th birthday in December, a week and a half before the Rose Bowl.

HUMPING DAY AND NIGHT

At the Airmen's Club you could always find decent food and cheap beer. On your birthday, they gave you a free bottle of champagne. A buddy from New Jersey and also a Lackland Air Force Base tech school classmate, Ron Timmons, and a couple of other guys agreed to help me celebrate the occasion.

We hit the club and I hit the bottles. It was fun! Why stop at one? I didn't. Ron caught a buzz, too, but was smart and reasonable about all the merriment. Me? Not so much. I didn't drink any booze through a straw, but the enjoyment ended abruptly when I noisily vomited across the table. Management threw us out and Ron helped me stagger back to the barracks, which thankfully was nearby.

Next thing I remember was sitting on the floor of the shower, cold water bouncing off my head and chest, clothes on and the room spinning. So this was what it meant to get plastered. What a mess. Ron helped me climb in my bunk and it was lights out. The next day was the opposite of pretty, but boy, what a friend I had from Jersey!

With months of humping aircraft under my belt, a big change was in the works. Within a day or so of OSU's Rose Bowl victory, the first sergeant called me into his office. Uh oh, being singled out. What the heck is this about?

"Airman Brown, you've done a nice job on security and we think you can take on more responsibility. We are going to reassign you and in a few days transfer you to Town Patrol in Taichung. Congratulations."

Wow, what had I done to get this? Well, I did do my job well and I made sure to always look sharp in uniform while doing it. These efforts apparently paid off. I had just been handed the most primo and prestigious duty for a sky cop at CCK.

I would be working in law enforcement with Chinese civilian and military police, I'd be living downtown off base and I'd be getting a boost in pay for expenses. I didn't know exactly why I got picked for this, but I jumped at the opportunity.

9
TAKING CARE OF BUSINESS

ON JANUARY 9, gear packed, I caught a ride to my new living quarters, the Hostel, where about a dozen security police on Town Patrol called home. Compared to the austere barracks I had just left, this place was downright extravagant.

Each room had space enough for a bed, table, desk, dresser, closet and large window. The Hostel served food and we all had Chinese house boys who made up the room, shined our shoes, did our laundry and would run errands. It was like living in a hotel with free room service! Talk about moving up.

Taichung Armed Forces Police—usually known as TAFP—was set up at the nearby Headquarters Support Activity Detachment 3 Compound, commonly known as the Navy Compound.

It was situated in a corner of a Chinese army base and surrounded by a six-foot stone wall. Inside was a small department-like store called a BX (Base Exchange), a liquor store, modest commissary, a four-lane bowling alley, a small theater and a government vehicle gas station.

We worked out of a small, white and gray rectangular cinder-block headquarters. A square-shaped room lay just inside the front door where a desk sergeant, or anyone of us, could type up incident and accident reports.

I quickly learned to be observant and carefully articulate everything in the incident and accident reports I had to write up nearly every day. I had no idea at the time, but this was excellent early training for my later-in-life career as a newspaper journalist.

To the left of the front door was a tiny barred cell with an uncomfortable, steel-framed lumpy bed, covered by a ratty green wool blanket. It was a temporary home to stash the people we had to put in handcuffs. They cooled their heels and tempers (sometimes) in that cell after they were arrested until we could transport them to CCK. A single bathroom was located to the right.

In the back another room held a few rows of filing cabinets and a large wall-mounted map of Taichung City, our reference for addresses when we were called out to respond to trouble in whatever form. It was also an office for the boss, known as the NCOIC—non-commissioned officer-in-charge. As hot and humid as it could get, we had no central air, but the front and back offices both had overworked, noisy and seemingly on-their-last-legs window air conditioners.

TAFP was comprised of a motivated, tight-knit group of guys who took the job of law enforcement seriously. Pretty much everyone on the team, including me, assumed a Town Patrol Swagger. We all thought we were bad asses and we played it off well. We didn't sweat nothin', but you kind of had to act the part to survive.

Maybe some of it was false bravado, but for me, I welcomed the uncommon feeling of confidence and the connection I formed with these guys. In just a short time, they became my away-from-home family. We looked out for and cared for one another, a bond made stronger by the sometimes-risky requirements of the job we had to do every day.

TAKING CARE OF BUSINESS

A central part of our work was on the Dirty Dozen, seven nights a week. Mix excitable, young, restless, looking-for-any-kind-of action airmen, alcohol and who-knows-what kind of drugs, and all manner of mischief would and did ensue. Toss in a bunch of guys who dropped in on a week's leave from humping the jungles of Vietnam for months, here to blow off steam on R&R, and you could guarantee fireworks.

Part of our job was to walk into the bars on patrol, looking for brewing trouble and half-to-fully inebriated Americans who may have passed out—a regular occurrence. We often ran into both.

We were usually a team of four—two Air Force security policemen, a Chinese local cop from a unit known as the Foreign Affairs Police (FAP) and a Chinese military police officer. We Americans had no firearms but we did pack a holstered black baton, a pair of handcuffs and our wits—that was it.

The Chinese cops were better equipped and they didn't play around either. They were rough on crime suspects. One local cop in particular, Sgt. Po-shen Lin, had a sweet, friendly disposition and he spoke English very well. But the man did hate pimps. We watched in shock once when he snatched one up by the belt and dangled him over a bridge railing. Well, it wasn't a high bridge. Anyway, on bar checks one of us Americans stood by the entrance to keep an eye on our partner as he walked casually through the bar, greeting mama-san and eyeballing the GIs. Our entrance into an establishment usually dampened the excitement level a notch or so and sometimes it ratcheted up the tension in the room.

When I first started doing these patrols, I was pretty jacked up myself on adrenaline and trepidation. It was a surreal feeling.

I'd never done anything even remotely close to this. Every eyeball in the room turned our way, putting us in the spotlight like we were some kind of unwelcome act.

It was uncomfortable in the first few weeks—the unknown, the unconventionality and the uncertainty of what might or what could happen next.

But soon enough I got used to these bar patrols and actually began to enjoy the role of being the town sheriff, so to speak. Part of that walk-through included entering the bathroom to see if anyone had lost consciousness. We found zonked out Americans once in a while. It was partly a quick sanitation check also, to ensure bars of soap, towels and toilet paper were on hand. Our Chinese compatriots usually milled around, chatting up the help and perhaps acquiring intel.

We parked our gray paddy wagons on the bar strip every night. The vehicles were squat Navy Ford Econovans, with four windows per side and "Armed Forces Police" lettered in black underneath. Rear doors opened to a well-used, musty cage in the back. A single, old-fashioned cherry red revolving light topped it all off. One favorite parking spot was just outside the 24-hour P.C.S. Snack Bar on Wu Chan Lu in the heart of the bar district. The restaurant excelled with its fried rice dishes, fried chicken and French fries and was advertised as a place "just like home." Our job was never boring, but more on that in a minute. I bonded quickly with this group of cops and one or two individuals in particular.

T.Sgt. Harry R. Eaton, of Queens, New York, was the TAFP boss at the time. Harry was a slender white guy, over six feet tall with dark, receding crew-cut hair and a long face ending in a square chin and cheeks that furrowed when he smiled. We might have said he slightly resembled Tom Cruise, had Cruise been around at the time. I took to this man like I would an admired older brother—and he was 14 years older. He became a mentor. He set the bar that I followed going forward—no bullshit and nose to the grindstone while on the job; after duty ended, and speaking of bars, it was "let's get this party started."

Harry would invite us to his room after work for some bullshit sessions, rock-'n'-roll music and cocktails. More than once, that group would saddle up and taxi over to the Dozen. It was how we lived our after-duty hours.

Alvin Hoover was the other major influence on me. Al was a skinny-as-a-rail Black kid from Lexington, North Carolina, with a quick and easy smile. He had been on Town Patrol for a while by the time I arrived and, as a partner, he helped me acclimate to the job.

We hit it off, worked well as a team and started having a few drinks after work with the other guys in the Hostel. We too would often end up going out to hit a few of the bars that we regularly patrolled.

Becoming friends with Al led to a life-changing experience. With no real intent, he bestowed on me a nickname—TC—and from that I developed a whole new persona. It began on a let's-hit-the-town kind of night.

In late 1968, a soundtrack was released that was cut from a U.S. TV special featuring the soul groups The Supremes and The Temptations. The album was released with a popular acronym at the time: *TCB—Takin' Care of Business.*

Al took the initials of my name, Terry Brown, and inserted the letter "C" in the middle, which was not part of my name, but which fit the times and our activities.

"Hey TCB, let's go TCB," he'd say.

I immediately knew the translation: "Time to get out and raise a little hell and have some fun!"

I liked it. From childhood I had never been fond of my name, Terry. And it was short for my actual full name, Terrence, which truly appalled me at the time. Sorry Mom and Dad.

While the Air Force considered Terrence to be my official name, none of my buddies called me that or Terry, either. "Brownie," on the other hand, was tossed out regularly. Didn't like that either. But now, thanks to my buddy Al, I had a brand new and very cool nickname!

The other guys on Town Patrol picked up on it quickly, but shortened it by dropping the "B." Thus, TC became my new identity. I'm convinced my development of character centered around those initials and their connotation helped crack the shell of shyness and standoffishness that had been an integral part of me since childhood.

Now I was unique. No name, just initials that changed my frame of reference and offered a little mystique. I liked it, a lot.

Over the ensuing years many people expressed curiosity about those initials and some, believing I was putting on airs, were dismissive. At first I told the true story. But that tale always felt a little too long and in reality, it was only meaningful to me. So over time I adopted an idea from the main character in John Irving's 1978 novel *The World According to Garp*.

The book's hero, T.S. Garp, hated people asking what his initials meant, so he made up stories about it. I didn't really mind queries, unless that was the first question out of a new acquaintance's mouth.

But I did find it fun and easier to make up stuff. I've tried on many different stories over the years. The best, usually drawing raised eyebrows and a quick laugh, was telling questioners that I was an unexpected surprise so my parents named me Terrence Clarence.

"They were real jokers. But you can just call me Terry Clary, if you like," I'd say.

Again, sorry Mom and Dad.

When I reflect back though, my personality metamorphosis probably began to take hold in tech school in Lackland before I met Al. Music was the spark of that transformation then, too. Every day the Black airmen in the barracks—the soul brothers—blasted out the funky melodies at the center of their culture, typically called soul music then, an urban and more commercial style of rhythm and blues.

The throbbing beat of the songs was always in the groove, which I intuitively picked up after seven years of drumming. As a music-crazed guy anyway, the mostly new-to-me unique sound and beat struck a deep internal chord.

It wasn't that I'd never heard soul music. Some artists like the Jackson 5 had already found success with crossover hits enjoyed by White audiences. There were Sly and the Family Stone's "Dance to the Music," "I Heard it Through the Grapevine," by Gladys Knight and the Pips, Jerry Butler's "Only the Strong Survive," or "It's Your Thing" by the Isley Brothers.

But now, through more exposure as barracks mates tried to drown out the sounds played by other guys down the hall, I was gaining a new appreciation and perspective of all this music and

Black culture. And even though I was White and pretty much clueless about my Black associates, I felt like I could relate through these tunes.

Before the military, I had barely exchanged a dozen words with Black people, let alone known anyone from the culture. Neither my high school or neighborhood included people of color.

Because of television I was vaguely aware of the Civil Rights Movement in the 1950s and 1960s, but this was my first real experience with Black society, thanks to the guys around me. I was fascinated and wanted to know more because this was alien to me, but I felt at least on some level—we're all human?—a kinship of sorts.

To be honest, I was not sure why. But I did know that when I cranked up the tunes popular with my soul brother peers, my body automatically began to sway, my shoulders and arms shimmied and my legs and feet got busy stepping, getting down on the beat. I could feel it, like Archie Bell & the Drells would sing in "Tighten Up:" ". . . we dance just as good as we walk."

Through soul music, I began to make a connection to this other culture that has lasted a lifetime. I didn't know these artists well, but I felt at home listening to James Brown screech out "Mother Popcorn," Mel & Tim harmonize on "Backfield in Motion" or The Impressions sing "A Better Day is Coming" in the song "Choice of Colors."

Over time Eddie Holman's "Hey There Lonely Girl," The Originals "Baby, I'm For Real" and The Friends of Distinction singing "Going In Circles" were tunes that deepened my connection with these unfamiliar but really cool guys around me.

I couldn't explain that connection but I felt the love expressed

TAKING CARE OF BUSINESS

so well by these musicians. If only music could somehow link all humanity on a grander scale and calm the racial animosity that rages just as badly today as it did in the 1960s.

I'm not sure how that would work or what that might look like, but I know taking the time to hear one another is a required first step, for sure. It's pretty clear there's not enough listening happening now, even as it was then.

Some of these insights would help save my own skin later on as racial hostilities grew.

10

DROPPING DRAWERS, LOSING FACE

BEING ON TOWN PATROL also taught me a lot more about another unfamiliar-to-me culture—Asian. We worked closely with Chinese police officers and our work space was Taichung and the surrounding area, so we were exposed to and interacted with the local population and their customs every day. It was quite an eye-opening experience and there was much to learn about their traditions.

As an added bonus, this was the best duty you could get as a cop when stationed at CCK. We lived and worked off base and were paid a per diem because of it. We didn't even have to drive in the early days. A couple of Chinese military guys chauffeured us around, sort of like a Stone Age Uber.

We'd wait out in front of the Hostel under the portal on the half-curved driveway. The drivers picked us up in the Econovan for a lift to our headquarters in the Navy Compound. Sometimes we'd kill time before a shift with the Chinese cops playing Sevens, an easy, fun card game that required a winner to play all of his cards. It was a small thing but speaking of customs, the game often kicked off with disagreements because the Asians wanted to play counter clockwise, the opposite of how we typically started games.

Year-round we dressed in a summer uniform—a short-sleeved khaki shirt and pants known as 1505s. We clipped a silver police badge to a button over our left shirt pocket. But a standout emblem compared to our Air Force peers, and a unique part of our uniform that was a real source of pride and coolness for us, was the armband that we wore on our left arm sleeve. It was black and gold with a gray patch and a snap at the bottom.

The top of it, however, required a safety pin to attach to our shirt sleeves. The patch had a small banner with the letters TAFP at the crown above what one can only assume was an eagle but looked more like a gray robin with large wings. The bird was perched on a box-like outline with the image of a police badge inside. Two sets of crossed rifles lay to the left of the badge and an anchor with USN stitched across it and clasped hands were to the right of the badge insignia.

"Republic of China" was written at the bottom of the box containing the badge. Underneath those images, the words "Taichung Armed Forces Police" in gold appeared above characters in Chinese that translated to "American Military Policeman."

We wore white, round military hats and carried a black baton and handcuffs on our black belts. The Chinese did not want Americans, even cops, carrying firearms off base, so while the Chinese MPs were armed, we were not. The civilian police carried innocent-looking metal batons that were about the size of a corn cob when retracted.

But when the officer pressed a lever, a metal baton shot out with substantial force, making it a formidable weapon that could be used to whack the bejesus out of the bad guys. I've seen video of police in the U.S. today using the very same style batons to bust through vehicle windows.

We worked hard and we partied hard. Being the law, we could stretch the envelope of foolishness and often enough we did stuff we would have arrested someone else for. Talk about abuse of power. For instance, there was the time myself and one of our crazy guys from Army STRATCOM—and they all seemed a little bit extreme—clambered atop a parked vehicle to see who could push the other off first.

Army Strategic Command had the top-secret job on the island of monitoring all kinds of broadcast transmissions, most likely from China, and they too liked to blow off steam. The STRATCOM guys also had rooms in the Hostel, were usually fun to hang out with and we liked them a lot, so we cut them slack if they went a little too far. You know, like climbing up on a car for a pushing contest—that kind of stupid thing. I'm not sure why we acted like buffoons but it was a friendly, not angry, match-up to see which idiot could stand up on the car the longest.

A mixture of our guys and their guys cheered us on like it was some kind of crucial, life-and-death gladiator battle. We shoved and huffed and pushed and grabbed and slipped, but somehow both of us managed to hold our own.

I have no idea why neither of us went flying off that car but in reality we weren't really trying too hard or for too long and we somehow managed to help each other stay upright. A wiser head in the crowd coaxed us both down without any broken limbs. It won't be a surprise to learn that alcohol fueled that mischief and many other such misadventures. Those Army guys took to us, likely in no small part because we offered them some cover.

Another cop who became a good friend and a partner was Ulysses Bryant, a wiry, 6'1" Black man from Savannah, Georgia, who we often called "Uly." He and I survived many skirmishes and a party life tinged with foolishness. One night he was hammered enough to think it was a great idea to jump on the back of a motorcycle with one of the STRATCOM guys as the dude drove it up a long flight of outdoor steps.

Once sober, Uly swore off ever trying that stunt again but it was fun to witness. We probably went too far off duty on many occasions because the work could be taxing and sometimes downright dangerous. Uly had come to Taiwan after working on Boston Armed Forces Police in Massachusetts, so my man already had some hard-earned experience with servicemen and alcohol.

For instance, one night he cautioned me to ignore my instincts to immediately dash into the middle of a large, ongoing brawl outside of a bar, with bodies and fists flying everywhere.

"We're not charging into that damn fight," he said. "Someone's gonna get knocked down and tossed out and we'll drag 'em out when they're too tired to fight anymore."

Every night was dynamic and different. It was a rare night to be bored. Most times you could count on some bad and unhinged incidents with a drunk American at the center of the action.

We were a nightly fixture, if not walking through the bars, we were hanging by the van at the bustling center of it all—bar girls, street vendors and CCK airmen seeking fun and excitement. We were a silent, visible presence of authority, a reminder to potentially rowdy Americans we were nearby, so best behave. Most times, it had little if any effect. It was not unusual for the trouble to come directly to us.

One night, after Uly and I had completed a couple of bar patrols, we were sitting in the van, cooling our heels and watching the usual assortment of characters pass by. It was quiet and around

DROPPING DRAWERS, LOSING FACE

10 p.m. when we noticed a rising commotion across the street, about 100 yards to our left. We saw a small crowd of Chinese gesturing as their voices grew louder. The fuss was also attracting the attention of other local passersby who joined the growing throng to see what was happening.

Uly, our Chinese partners and I jumped out of the van and started to move toward the pack. A figure broke out of the gathering and began running in our direction, but still across the street. At least a half dozen or more people, yelling loudly now, began to give chase.

That sparked us into action and we began sprinting across the street in the direction of this developing melee. This looked to turn into a crazy bad situation very quickly.

Before we could intersect the crowd, one of the Chinese pursuers, wielding a long bamboo stick, swiped the runner's legs, bringing him down. Luckily for him, we were close enough by now to see it was an American on the ground.

Our arrival put the brakes on the crowd and likely kept people from jumping him and kicking the crap out of him. The Chinese hitter turned tail and ran off in the other direction. The dude on the ground was clearly happy to see us.

"These guys are trying to kill me," he breathlessly shouted as he struggled to his feet.

Some of the Chinese were chattering loudly to our native law enforcement colleagues who tried to calm the group, which continued to point and curse at the American.

I could smell alcohol and see his eyes were bloodshot as we asked for his ID and questioned him, attempting to sort out the hubbub.

"My friends and I were just walking down the street, minding our own business and these guys started yelling at us," he said, weaving slightly. "I don't know if they were wanting to rob us or what.

"I told them to fuck off and get out of the way and they started coming after me," he said.

We wondered what crucial details were being left out.

As his two buddies milled about, looking at the ground and nodding, our Chinese partners were getting the other side of the story. It turned out to be quite a different tale, no surprise.

"Uh, TC, this old man say he walking down street on way home when this American come up behind, pull his undershorts down to ground," Sgt. Lia-hua Chen of the Foreign Affairs Police said. "He wear nothing underneath. This very embarrassing! He lose face. This serious."

He certainly lost more than face, but Chen wasn't kidding. First off, the Chinese put their elders on a pedestal. They are revered and respected for their wisdom. Senior citizens are not left in old folks' homes; families care for their older relatives who live with them until they die. When they're gone, the family honors them with altars in the home that include photographs, candles and the deceased's favorite items.

Second, Taiwan gets steamy hot in the summer, with temperatures that average in the 90s. Many Chinese, including the older folk, walk around in T-shirts and undershorts, with nothing on underneath. Going commando, in other words. The airman and his buddies sheepishly changed their tune when we relayed the old man's version of the story.

"We had a few drinks and were going to another bar when I saw papa-san in front of me in his undies," the perpetrator said. "I thought it would be funny to give his shorts a little tug, that's all. I didn't know they would come all the way off."

Uly and I struggled to suppress laughter. This thing could have been a whole lot worse. The customary "bottoms up" for this drunk had turned into "bottoms out." Our Chinese partners were not amused. They demanded action.

We cuffed the airman and charged him with drunk and disorderly conduct. We deposited him in the cage in the back of the van and pulled away, bound for the near-bare cell in our Navy Compound headquarters.

Major misadventure and any injuries were averted and papa-san's dignity was restored a little with the arrest, hopefully.

11
TYPHOONS AND TRAINS

NOT EVERY CONFRONTATION was amusing, weird or with minimal damage, albeit losing face in Asia is not taken lightly, ever. You pretty much, however, could always count on stupid entering the picture when it came to partying young airmen. And stupid takes many forms

For some, booze provides a sense of invincibility and toughness, as we continued to learn week after week. We could bank on intoxicated Americans testing us on a routine basis. Every time I had to confront a big drunk guy, I immediately went on alert, nerves jangling.

It was hard enough trying to corral a wild, out-of-control average-size person. I was short with a little pudge around the middle and with arms like swollen cannoli's, filled with cream, not muscle. Few, if any, used a gym in those days, and I was certainly no pioneer in that arena.

With my size, I wasn't much of an intimidating force, so it was always good to have a partner and that black truncheon. On one domestic disturbance call, I responded with my roommate and partner Jarema Mykitscahk, who we took to calling "Myk" because, well, it was just easier. He and I had about the same build.

As we clomped up several flights of apartment stairs, we heard loud yelling coming from one apartment. We banged on the door which soon was whipped open by an obviously trashed American, a pretty large American at that. After some brief discussion, we told him he would have to come with us. He sneered and said, "You guys aren't big enough to take me in."

He might have been right, but we were the law and we weren't about to argue the point, no matter what was about to occur. So, without words and almost as if on cue, Myk and I both unholstered our night sticks. With raised eyebrows and before we could take any action, the big guy said, "OK, OK, I'll go."

That was an easy one and not totally unusual. Sometimes our willingness to use force got through to a troublemaker before we actually had to act.

After a couple of months on Town Patrol I had discovered an ironic twist in this down-and-dirty police grind. The massive guys often were the most compliant, thankfully. They'd tend to listen to reason, if not too smashed.

The bantam boys? Always ready to put up their dukes and dare you to tell them what to do. It didn't matter what the occasion was, even if you were trying to take them out of danger—like from a "Super Typhoon" with winds peaking at 175 miles per hour.

Taiwan sits in a region known by climatologists as "Typhoon Alley." The western Pacific basin experiences some of Earth's most ferocious storms and Typhoon Elise, which formed over the Western Pacific on Sept. 19, 1969, was no exception.

It grew in size, bearing down on the island, hitting its top-speed winds five days later. The base evacuated aircraft and began to batten down operations and everything else that moved or could be moved by wild wind.

TYPHOONS AND TRAINS

The base commander recalled all airmen to CCK before this monster hit. Town Patrol's job was to cruise through all of the bars, tell the American patrons to hustle back home and make sure the establishments had locked their doors. Making life more complicated for us was that Elise would hit Taiwan on Friday the 26th. And guess what young guys want to do on Fridays?

I was partnered with S.Sgt. Ike Chavez, a fastidious dresser from Albuquerque, New Mexico, who wore his white hat with its normally round inside liner crushed in toward his face, giving it a suave, curved form. Chavez constantly flashed a wide smile under his thick, dark mustache. We nicknamed him "Cisco" and he was a cool customer, yes, but also no nonsense.

As the tropical storm worked its way toward the island, Chavez and I along with our Chinese partners herded out the few remaining patrons on the bar strip who pined for that last pre-typhoon pint. Winds and rain had already begun to whip down Wu Chan Lu as we worked our way through the last line of saloons.

As the bearers of bad news, we were an unwelcome sight in every establishment. Fortunately, word of the return order had already circulated and most places held only a few customers, if any, and they were cooperative.

Well, almost everyone. One diminutive guy, sitting alone in the Ruby Club, took the road less traveled.

"Hey buddy, you've got to clear out and head back to the base, the bar is closing" Chavez said, coming up to the guy on his left as he sat at the bar. I approached him from behind on the other side.

The drinker simply sat on the barstool, not moving, not talking, not drinking. Uh oh. We knew he wasn't deaf and we weren't invisible, so that left one prospect—trouble.

"Hey man, did you hear me?" Chavez asked, I thought politely enough. "You have to leave now and get back to the base. The typhoon's gonna hit soon and everybody's been called back. So get moving!"

"I'm good. I'll be fine here," the guy said, looking at us through the bar mirror attached to the back wall. "Besides, I haven't finished my drink."

Chavez looked at me, turned back to the guy and said, "You're either leaving on your own now, or we're hauling you out of here in cuffs."

Like I said, no nonsense.

The only movement was the guy shrugging his shoulders. It appeared things were about to "get down," but not in a way usually expressed in a soul song.

Chavez glanced at me and nodded toward the guy, wordlessly transmitting the next move. He reached out and grabbed the dude's left arm. I was a half second behind as I reached for his right, but he swung up and away, knocking my hat to the floor.

I caught his wrist just as he pushed off against the bar with his feet, launching himself and his barstool backwards toward us. With a noisy crash, the stool smacked the floor.

The girls and mama-san screamed, backing away as the three of us lurched backward into a table against the wall, which also crashed to the ground along with the three of us falling on top of it.

TYPHOONS AND TRAINS

Oh, it was definitely "on." The scuffle quickly turned into an old West bar brawl. Glassware shattered, tables and chairs tumbled and broke and women screeched in fright.

Chavez and I clamped on this guy's arms like our lives depended on it. He was either the strongest little man I'd encountered or he was so trashed he felt no pain—maybe both. Just another real-life lesson learned in patrolling the streets of Taichung.

We kept wrestling the guy on the floor with him between us. He twisted, kicked and arched his body, trying to shake us off. He fought like a demon. We finally twisted his arms up behind him—that good old police arm bar—and got him cuffed.

We hauled him to his feet, but at this point we were all sucking air, in dire need of oxygen. And Chavez and I were pissed—real pissed. We were banged up and out of breath because this clown had to keep drinking, even as a typhoon bore down on his dumb ass.

He kept fighting as we struggled to get him out through the front door. Once outside, Chavez glanced at me and then down at the guys legs. Got it. We each swiped a leg and took his feet out from under him.

The rain had been falling now for a while, creating puddles and turning the ground into muck. We grabbed his handcuffed arms and drug the idiot, front-side down, through the mud and water until we could get the back door open and toss him inside the van's cage.

Next stop for the troublemaker? The holding cell back at the Navy Compound. He gave us a workout just before this monster of a typhoon slammed into the city, creating havoc on the base and around the entire island. That storm killed 105 people, knocked out power and water for a few days across Taiwan and ripped off roofs and flattened bus stops. I'm sure the tough guy didn't appreciate our rescue, but regardless, he remained our guest until we could safely transport him to CCK.

Thankfully, typhoons were not a consistent adversary for us, but dealing with injuries and the occasional loss of life was definitely a large part of our Town Patrol duties. Along with patrolling bars, corralling drunks and breaking up fights, responding to a never-ending stream of traffic accidents on the island was a mainstay of this work. No wonder. The streets were constantly crammed with movement, in all forms—vehicle, pedestrian and animal.

That traffic included slow strolling, sometimes aggressive water buffalo ambling down the roadway in front of their owners, competing for space with cars, buses, scooters and a steady stream of pedicab-for-hire guys. These strong-legged bicyclists peddled passengers on a couch-like seat anchored on a carriage attached to the rear of their bikes. In some of our dodgy off-duty moments a couple of us would rent pedicabs and urge the drivers with a little extra cash to race one another. Luckily no human or street animal was ever injured in these goofy competitions. Contributing to the craziness on the roads was a seeming lack of—or maybe it was simply disregard for—any rules. Taxi drivers were the worst. To operate a taxi in Taiwan required only two qualifications—drive like a maniac and rely on "a margin of safety" of about two inches.

More than one driver turned to me in the back seat after stomping his brakes through the floor to stop just shy of a seemingly unavoidable crash.

TYPHOONS AND TRAINS

"No sweat man, lots room," he'd say, smiling widely and holding up a slightly parted thumb and index finger.

Tell that to my racing heart, locked-up muscles and frozen breath.

No harm done, true enough, but their margin of safety did not instill confidence. And it didn't always work, so we were dispatched on a regular basis to investigate traffic accidents involving Americans and Chinese. It could be a weird and sometimes gruesome experience.

We'd pull up on a crash with just a few people milling around. Soon after, the area would be swarming with Chinese most likely interested in checking out the commotion and the foreign cops first hand. Some accidents were little more than fender benders; some we witnessed were grim scenes. But no accident, for me, topped the guy on the train—the top of the train, that is.

Some local Chinese police from up the island called our office one morning to say a farmer had found an American body lying out in a rice paddy north of Taichung and south of Taipei. In other words, out in the boondocks. How in the heck did that happen, if it really was an American?

I happened to be working the day shift, a rare occurrence, when that call came in. Usually only one patrolman and a desk sergeant worked in the daytime. Pretty much the rest of the crew came in for the nightly swing shift, when most of the action occurred.

This was an out-of-the-ordinary call so a Chinese counterpart and myself were dispatched to investigate this mysterious death. If this was an American, we had to recover the body and bring it back to Taichung. And we had to try to figure out how he ended up out in the middle of nowhere.

It was an extraordinary incident from our normal duty and we had no idea what to expect. With guidance from the local cops, we made arrangements for a Chinese ambulance to meet us and we motored north for the nearly two-hour trip.

The location of the corpse was definitely in the backwater. We had to work our way carefully and slowly through many narrow, remote farm lanes, more accustomed to water buffalo than a Navy Econovan.

The local cops were waiting on us and by their raised eyebrows, wide smiles and the once over I got, they seemed intrigued to see an American of any stripe. We had pulled up near a small bridge over a tunnel, which was large enough to enfold two sets of railroad tracks. A rickety looking farm truck was parked to the side of the road, belonging to the driver who had discovered the body.

The locals chattered with my partner and motioned for us to follow them. They gave us a wallet they found on the body with an Air Force ID. In the back of my mind I had been hoping someone was mistaken about his nationality, but no more.

We stepped into the rice field at the side of the railroad tracks and waded through several inches of water and mud, trying to step over and around the above-ankle green shoots of rice. We didn't go far before we saw the body. As we walked up, we could see it was dressed in civilian clothes.

He was stiff, bloated and reeked. The corpse was still in a state of rigor mortis. I wondered if the bloat was because his body had absorbed the field water around it. It was clear the man had been dead for a while.

He was tough to look at, too. A violent force had caved in the right side of his face and head. My stomach started churning in somersaults and I had to step away and take some deep breaths.

The Chinese police said they were unable to find any other evidence on or around the body and neither did we. A medic unzipped a body bag and with some difficulty, we wrestled the man inside.

Six of us grabbed handles on the side of the now weighty bag and tramped our way through the field muck to muscle the body into the back of the ambulance. It was only upon our return to Taichung that we got the full story, which came from his buddy who was with him when he was killed.

Both Americans had spent a couple of days in Taipei, sightseeing and partying hearty. They carried on the merrymaking up until the time of departure at the train station that evening. Both had tickets for seats for the three-hour trip. But for some reason, perhaps the adventure of it, they decided to ride back home "on" the train, literally.

They managed to clamber up on top of one of the cars where they lay flat. It was a risky and dangerous perch just for some kicks and to return to Taichung in style, carrying back an outlandish story.

All went well for about half of the trip until the now-dead guy got the urge for a cigarette. As the train moved along the rail, slowing down slightly, he leaned up a bit to get a lighter out of his pocket.

Bam! The train had just entered a tunnel. There was no room for his head and the impact launched the man off the car and out into the field. I can only imagine the terror experienced by his companion who rode the rest of the way by himself back to Taichung.

I also felt sorry for the dead guy's family and I often wondered how or if the Air Force described the specifics of the accident to them. What a loss.

12
IN FOR A PENNY

THE DIRTY DOZEN was party central for many American airmen stationed at CCK. It was the "hot spot" and a place to explore new-found sexual freedom, besides being the place where the proverbial shit hit the fan regularly.

We knew and understood both of these elements well because of all the hours we spent on that bar strip every day, working and having off-duty fun ourselves. So it was only a matter of time that once the Air Force assigned me to Town Patrol, I would fall for one of the women who worked in one of the bars.

By this time, I was a free man relationship-wise. After I jettisoned my virginity on that first night in town I had been driven by a rushing river of guilt. In my strict Catholic upbringing, sex before marriage was at the top of the sin hit parade and the equivalent of a major felony. I struggled with this moral conflict and ultimately decided I had to come clean and confess.

Against the robust advice from my buddies, I had written what had to have been a heart-shattering letter to Rebecca, my girl in Ohio. In it, I confessed the sin of cheating on her, although I'm pretty sure I left out the part that it happened within a day of my arrival in Taichung.

I was no longer a virgin and I don't remember the words I actually wrote, but I know I expressed sorrow at my infidelity and pledged it would never happen again. I'm sure that was believable as hell! That letter had to deliver a gut-busting, harsh blow to her. Up until then we had written to each other regularly.

I had even called her a couple of times through the MARS ham radio-call link to home, not realizing then the hidden and literal meaning of using the word "over" in those conversations with her. I should have expected Rebecca's next move after my confession letter, but I hoped she might forgive me since I was being honest now. Maybe everything could still work out. Either naïveté continued to rule my thinking or I was in denial about how the world worked. Most likely it was a fusion of both.

Not long after my correspondence to Rebecca, she dropped a Dear John missive on my butt. The end had come to pass. Who could blame her? She had to have been seriously hurt and that "Dear John" goodbye letter was our last communication.

Selfishly, and ridiculously in hindsight, I felt hurt, sad and even a little let down myself. Heavy regret set in. Some of that remorse was the moral struggle—I had cheated on her and broken a solemn promise. And speaking of moral struggle, I was also disappointed and kicking myself that I didn't listen to my friends' sage advice not to write that letter in the first place. I was turning my back on honesty even as my Catholic guilt was in full bloom in my head.

It took some time, but thankfully personal decency won out and I eventually came to understand how wrong it was to so easily toss aside a commitment pledge to someone, and that in the end it was right to be honest with her about my unfaithfulness.

Nonetheless, for a while I was miserable and I began to

drown that gloom with alcohol. I was developing an appetite for the booze, even beer, which had made me puke my guts out and flattened me with a hangover in high school.

Within about a month or so of going on Town Patrol, I wandered into the Flying Tiger Restaurant on Ta Ya Road, which had a bar, live music, a pool table and which advertised: "So many attractions to the customers." I certainly found one diversion.

One night when I was off duty, I entered the dimly lit tavern, juke box blaring the songs of the day. As I sat on a stool, I looked across the bar and spotted a slender young woman with large eyes and long dark shiny hair, flowing past her shoulders.

She saw me looking and walked over.

"Ni hao ma," I said, greeting her with the Mandarin version of how are you? "Could I have an American beer?"

"OK," she replied, turning to get the beer.

I could see she was petite and pretty damn cute. She brought the beer and put it in front of me.

"What's your name?" I asked.

"Penny," she said, flashing a white-tooth smile over a small squared chin.

She was just over 5-feet tall, with prominent cheekbones, dark almond-shaped eyes and a button nose. Like all of the women employed in the bars, Su Chen had adopted an American first name, I guess to make us feel more at home and to make them fit in with our culture. I don't remember ever asking her why she chose Penny, but I was immediately smitten.

"I'm TC. Nice to meet you."

"TC? Your name, TC? OK," she said, laughing. "You MP, right? I see you come in, checkie, checkie every night."

Interesting to hear she recognized me but not totally surprising. She obviously knew who I was from our regular bar patrols. And that's how we started talking. I was fascinated and infatuated and my loneliness began to fade as I became a regular at the Flying Tiger Restaurant.

From this night on, every time we hit that joint on a patrol, threads of nervous excitement zipped through my gut because I would get to see her. As time went on, the other girls chattered at her when we swept in, likely giving her good-natured grief.

When we started dating I think she gained "face," a sense of standing because I represented local law enforcement. No doubt mama-san looked on the relationship kindly, and perhaps as a chit against the trouble that eventually crossed the doorstep of all of the Taichung bars.

This was my first relationship that was adult in the sense we began to "get it on," the common lingo for that sort of thing in those days. Fact is, other than my first sexual homerun that I paid for when I first got to the island, I had zero experience in that arena.

Penny was a little shy at first, too, but we worked at it and had fun learning together. She had a decent command of English, including reading and writing. But like many of her countrymen, she struggled with understanding some phrases, especially American slang like "give me some skin."

"You want my skin?" she asked the first time she heard it, laughing.

We spent a lot of time together, especially early on, as we were trying to figure one another out. It wasn't just the language barrier. Our cultures were vastly different in so many aspects and sometimes I had difficulty understanding what was going on with her. She had the same issues with me. She had a rocky early childhood, which had to be an influential factor in her personality.

She was only a year old when her parents split up. Her father's sister and brother-in-law had no kids, so they took her in instead of one of her parents, which was likely an intense emotional decision.

In Chinese society, girl babies held way less value compared to boys. The culture had a long history of parents abandoning daughters while treating their sons more favorably, even in terms of food and health care.

Sons were viewed as a "pension" for elders; girls were considered to be wasteful. Penny moved in with her aunt and uncle, but when she was three, her uncle passed away.

Penny developed a generous spirit and she hated to see people going hungry. She didn't talk much about her youth, but I'm guessing life was a bit of a struggle after her uncle died. She likely experienced some of that hunger in a poor family of two females. More than once, I watched her give money to or buy food for children, and she encouraged me to donate, too, which I did.

Her now-single aunt wasted no time turning Penny into a moneymaker when she got a little older. She yanked her out of 10th grade to start work as a waitress in a restaurant. That drastic decision was challenging for me to imagine.

She was 18 when we met and she had been baptized a Catholic three years before that. For me and my own dedicated faith, it was another connection that told me I was on the right track. Many of the natives I had encountered in Taiwan were Buddhists, so this was like an encouraging sign for me.

We began to take day trips outside of Taichung to visit beautiful parks a short distance away. We also ventured around the island, checking out popular spots like the picturesque Sun Moon Lake, or going even farther for weekends to the cosmopolitan capital of Taipei, often traveling with my TAPF buddies and their girlfriends.

Once we traveled into the country with one of my partners, John Williams, and his Chinese girlfriend, Katie, to a large, swiftly flowing stream. Finding extended walking sticks, the four of us waded out into the middle and plopped down on our butts, fully clothed, letting the chilling, rolling water rush rapidly over us. I wore a bamboo hat as sun protection, drawing ridicule at my attempt to look Chinese. I was assimilating the culture, or at least fantasizing I was.

I fell hard and fast for Penny. It was only much later in life that I came to understand falling in love at the drop of a dime was a pattern and my standard operating procedure. But Penny returned that love and need that I also felt.

The cost of living in Taiwan was way more inexpensive than back home, and I made enough money to afford an apartment outside of my room at the Hostel. I rented a small one in a large, multi-story building and we moved in together and she began to study English. On patrol, it was always difficult for me to see her talking and laughing with other guys in the Flying Tiger. I knew it was her job but I would tense up when I saw this. A streak of jealousy would zap me, which was stupid considering the kind of work she did. She knew how I felt, and when she saw our patrol enter the bar, she always made sure to look my way.

Whatever fun she was having with a stranger in front of her got toned down, at least until we walked back out. I always asked later who she was talking to and what they wanted from her. Duh!

The jealous ache I felt motivated me to get her out of the bar scene. She eventually quit working. That required me to give a payout to mama-san, but I no longer remember what that "dowry" was. But now Penny and I were really playing adult house, just like man and wife.

We had only been together for about four months when I decided I wanted to marry this young woman. She was beautiful and funny and unique and foreign to everything I had known.

It was exciting. It was an adventure and I was coming to realize I loved escapades. I was thousands of miles from home and family. I had been lonely but now I was not. Most of my life I had been uncommonly shy around girls. Now I was in a distinctive relationship. I asked her to marry me and she said yes. I was acting like an adult, but I was still young and unsophisticated.

Many Chinese did not like to see their women with an American. To them, it was a loss of respect and "face." Her aunt resisted our proposal so Penny had to work on her, though I have no idea what she promised. But Penny eventually won her approval. Now, it was my turn. I had to break the news to my parents, who had no clue about Penny or our love affair.

I put off telling them for a couple of months. I was scared about how my family would react. My parents weren't overtly racist, but they were old school and had some intolerable views about mixing cultures.

I needed their approval in a notarized letter because I was only 19 and was marrying a foreigner. Instead of an OK, I wondered if they might disown me.

Who knows how long I would have continued to put this off, but time was not on my side. My tour in Taiwan, even with a three-month extension, would come to an end in six months—February 1970. I was desperately trying to save money because we intended to get married before I left the island. I would ship back to the states and then send for her, wherever I ended up, and because we were married the process would be much easier. I was certainly not alone. I followed the road taken by many of my American comrades who also took Asian brides back home. Some stuck around and even today, decades later, maintain homes on the island.

I wrote a letter to Mom and Dad on Aug. 1, which I still have along with my parents' reply. In the first paragraph, I apologized for not writing for a while and then tried to prepare them for what they were about to read.

"I hope the news I tell you won't shock or surprise you too much, but I suppose it will so maybe you'd better be sitting when you read this."

Then I dropped the bomb.

"The news is that in either Nov or Dec I want to get married. I sure hope that everybody doesn't take the news too hard because I am really happy about it."

I didn't mention her name until the third paragraph when I told them that Penny "is one of the most wonderful people I've ever met." I also acknowledged the issues likely to arise. I knew it was a giant leap and one I didn't take lightly.

"I know that there will be a lot of problems, such as money, language barriers, her adjusting to the states, etc, etc.," I wrote. "But this isn't a one-day decision. I've thought and planned this for a couple of months . . . I've checked all the aspects and into some of the problems and I'm sure we could both make it."

I did not take a dive into what I thought the "aspects" and "problems" might be, but I told them I would not leave her behind when I came back.

"I want to spend my life with her."

I told my parents she "speaks real good English," a sentence structure that indicated I might not be so hot at it. I also offered a confession, which seemed to be a routine thing for me in Taiwan. Earlier that year I had asked them for $100 for stereo speakers, which they sent. I admitted I did it so I didn't have to dip into the money I had been saving to get married.

And in acknowledging I had put off writing this, I admitted to "being a chicken at heart." It wasn't my only cowardly omission. While I told them I had met her in a "restaurant," I neglected to mention she was working as a "bar girl."

I also enclosed a picture of the two of us wading in that heavy-flowing stream Penny and I had visited with me hanging onto a large walking stick, conical hat askew. In a postscript I said, "Dig the crazy Chinaman in the coolie hat."

That had to be unsettling.

I begged for their consent, ". . . that is if you don't want to kick me out of the family."

I sealed the letter and mailed it and held my breath.

In a reply dated Aug. 12, the day after they had received my jaw-dropper, my dad started his letter with "My Dear Son" and bluntly told me that he and my mother were not yet over the shock of my news.

He wrote that my grandmother and my aunt and uncle might "still be in orbit" over the newsflash. (It was the year of the Apollo moon flights.) He said he was writing this letter as a "joint venture" with my mom. He wanted me to read their reply with an open mind. Uh, oh.

"I told your mother earlier that I wish that I could have just a touch of the wisdom of Solomon so that I might write the correct words to you."

Surprisingly he admitted that as I grew up they may not have "always been fair" with me, but they had always tried hard to be honest, an attribute that they constantly encouraged me to adopt.

"I feel that now, we both would be less than honest if we told you that we were overjoyed to read of your wish to marry," he wrote. "Our objection to your proposed marriage is the fact that at nineteen, we feel you are much too young." He called my concern that they would boot me out of the family over this "absurd." And he wanted to know if I intended to go to college because without a degree I'd be "dead, dead, dead." My father did not attend college and one of his major regrets in life was that he did not have a university degree, believing it severely hindered his ability to earn.

"If I had completed college, my income would be more than double what it is now," he wrote. "Don't ever lose sight of that goal."

It was a common theme spoken by my dad throughout my childhood. Our family wasn't poor, but things were often pretty tight. And money, or lack thereof, was most often the central premise of any household strife.

He wanted to know how Penny might deal with homesickness or how we would deal "with any possible discrimination from our so-called countrymen?" Some things never change, I guess.

In truth, he made good points I hadn't thought much about. But he also wrote that they would consent to our marriage and "would love her as our own daughter." But before they would send a notarized letter they wanted to know her full American and Chinese names. They didn't realize they already had the full American name.

Their assent came with a price. I had to pledge to complete my college education and I had to promise not to have children until I was discharged from the Air Force. That last demand must have been a mountain for them. They were seriously practicing Catholics, which my dad acknowledged. But he was a realist and knew it would be challenging to support a family on military pay." Have you ever wondered why your Mom and Dad had only two children? We have always felt that it is a much greater sin to bring children into the world and then not be able to properly care for them," he said. And they were Republican, too!

This unforeseen jolt of news that their son was about to get married to a Chinese woman on the other side of the world surely generated a torrent of distress and worry.

"Make doubly certain this is what you want to do. It will be one of the most important decisions you will ever make."

Nonetheless, they assured me they would welcome Penny into the family. They were also sad that they would miss the wedding.

"Have lots of pictures taken, you hear?" And with one final appeal to "make doubly certain in your own mind that this is what you want to do," he mailed it.

My reaction reading their reply was mixed. I understood my letter caused angst at home, but my mind was made up. Penny would be my wife. I was happy to obtain my parent's consent, but I wasn't crazy about the required quid-pro-quo pledges. Although I didn't know what I didn't know in those days, I believed I was a grown man. I would do what was best for me.

Only much later did I appreciate how difficult this had to be for my parents. They wanted me to succeed, thus the demand for certain assurances. I'm sure they knew I might also rebel, like any young man my age. So I had their OK, but it was going to be difficult to get everything arranged before I was ordered back to the states in only a few months. And if I did not marry Penny before I left, I would face a mountain of obstacles to return to make this longing come true. What could I do to get more time?

After some thought, I hit on a nearly sure-fire way to ensure I could make it back to Taiwan.

I could volunteer to go to Vietnam.

13
DEATH DECISIONS

MY TOUR IN TAIWAN was up in February, but I had not yet received an assignment back to The World, the wistful designation every American serviceman in Asia called home. If I could stay in the Pacific theater, I was confident I could get back to the island. Vietnam was a voracious maw for young men, so I knew that already being so geographically close to that war, they'd likely snatch me up if I volunteered to go.

This path made the most sense to me. I would do a year in 'Nam and request a reassignment to CCK afterward. And I would still have 16 months left in the Air Force, enough time to complete another Taiwan stint.

It would not be a problem to save money living in a combat zone. And when I returned, we'd get married and have plenty of time to prepare for our return to the states. Perfect. I made a conscious decision not to dwell on the danger part. The head-in-the-sand part of me still ruled with a solid hold on my thought processes.

My new strategy was not received with joy.

"I no like this idea," Penny said, when I told her what I planned. "You go to Veetnam, you no come back."

"No, that's not true, honey," I said. "This will give us time to save money. That will help us a lot. We won't have to rush. We don't have enough time or money right now to get married in a couple of months."

"No, no good. Don't go. You go, you no come back," she pleaded.

I don't know if she meant "not come back" because I would abandon her or even worse, being that it was Vietnam.

We talked this over for the next couple of weeks and eventually she reluctantly accepted the inevitable. Even though countless servicemen had married local women, she had already seen too many Americans leave their girlfriends behind with promises to return that were never fulfilled. But I knew this was the way to go and my mind was made up. I volunteered and, no surprise, the military granted my request.

Now, instead of getting married in November, I received orders to report to the 6251st Security Police Squadron in the 3rd Combat Support Group at Bien Hoa Air Base in south-central Vietnam, 16 miles northeast of Saigon.

I was instructed to travel to Taipei for a flight out on Feb. 3, 1970. I knew I had to get back home to see my people once again during the holidays and on my 20th birthday in December before heading off to war, so I requested a month's leave.

Not only would I miss the Bob Hope tour that landed at CCK in December, I was leaving behind a sullen fiancée. I flew home for a whirlwind visit with family and friends.

Back home I took a few days to jump on a Greyhound Bus to visit my former mentor Harry Eaton, who was then at Griffiss Air Force Base in Rome, New York, northeast of Syracuse. It was a grueling 17-hour trip, made more awful after I laid my head against the back of the seat and it slid sideways from all the grease on the seat's cloth.

The return bus trip to Columbus was my last-ever Greyhound ride. Still, it was a memorable visit. Harry and I spent our time drinking, listening to our favorite songs of the day on the jukebox at the NCO club, or dropping in from the frigid winter weather to the local bars and reminiscing about our Town Patrol days in Taichung. Harry longed to go back.

He eventually did get back for a visit by doing what I did—volunteering for Vietnam. He ended up in Bien Hoa in 1971 after I had left, and he and I did reunite one more time when he later took his R&R from Vietnam to Taiwan. I have no idea how much my path eventually influenced his own, but his friendship over those years meant the world to me.

I didn't see Rebecca while in Columbus nor did I try. I heard she had a boyfriend and, still feeling guilt about what I did to her, I felt good about that. Enough tension was already circulating in my immediate family without trying to add a visit to the girl I had jilted. I had put off getting married but had not changed my mind about that decision. And I was headed to a war zone, though I still didn't dwell on the potential for a bad outcome. I'm sure the prospective hazards did cross the minds of my parents, grandma and brother. My father and I already had a long history of butting heads. We were both strong willed with each other. I know he loved me, and he and the rest of my family had to be worried for my safety. Both my mom and dad were in the Navy In World War II, so they knew some things about war.

Dad and I weren't estranged, but I had erected some defensive walls and I just didn't feel that close to him. The strain is evident in my face in the last picture he and I took together before I turned tail for Taiwan.

After a month's leave, during which the Air Force promoted me to sergeant, I flew back to Taiwan and CCK, with a few weeks of duty left before shipping out. I began to anxiously pack as I wondered what the coming days might bring in Vietnam. I was mentally gearing up for this next adventure when stunning news on the morning of January 30 changed it all. I was ordered to report to the security police commander's office on CCK. What now?

"At ease. Sit down, Sgt. Brown," Capt. David Billingsly said. "I'm afraid I have to give you some bad news. There's no easy way to say this. Your family called. Your father passed away yesterday."

A dark, swirling mist flooded my senses and the room disappeared. I sat stupefied, feeling lost and untethered from reality. Seemingly from a distance, I heard him mention "serious heart attack" and "sudden" and "died." He said other words, too, but I was dazed.

He sent me to the administration office to begin processing out for an emergency leave to return back home, which I had left just weeks before. Things moved so quickly, I barely had time to tell Penny, who was stunned and saddened by the rapid turn of events, as was I. "Trust me honey," I said, hands gripped loosely around her upper arms. "I am coming back for you and you will be my wife. Do you understand?"

She looked down and nodded her head, tears shining on her cheeks.

And with a hug and a long kiss, I left her and that beautiful island and headed to an unknown future.

DEATH DECISIONS

It was a brutally long flight to get back home; it took more than a day. To get me out as quickly as possible, they put me in the back of an Air Force plane. With the trauma of the situation and the uncomfortable red webbed, sidewall benches, I was unable to sleep or even sit comfortably for that dreadfully long trip.

It's all hazy, but I'm sure I spent those waking hours reflecting on the loss of my dad. He was strict and could be a tough guy, and as I had entered my teen years we had grown distant. I think I had lost some respect for him as time went on and now those feelings evoked waves of guilt and sorrow in the wake of his loss.

Despite the barrier that had grown between us, I nonetheless had no doubt that we both loved each other in our own ways, even if it was not always visible. But neither of us ever really said it. Now it didn't matter.

I made it back for his funeral and was home for nearly a month, but most of that time I was punch-drunk. Because of my changed circumstances, the Air Force offered an opportunity for me to seek a hardship reassignment to a base closer to home, like Wright Patterson Air Force Base in Dayton, instead of shipping me off to Vietnam.

It was an agonizing time for our family. Part of me wanted to stay around to help out. Afterall, my mom had only my 75-year old grandmother and my 13-year-old brother at home now.

But I had a fiancée in Taiwan who I loved and who I desperately wanted to be with. I knew by staying in the states, the chances of us getting married and having her come to the U.S. were slim at best. We talked it over several different times and my mother was always wise, brave and, of course, honest.

"Terry, you have to do what you think is best for you. If you feel like you have to go back, then you should go back. We will be fine," she told me in a frank conversation.

My mom, like my grandmother who raised three young children by herself after my grandfather left her in 1927, was a strong woman.

I was torn. I desperately wanted to go back to Asia but that fully-ingrained Catholic guilt also kicked in—leaving my family seemed to be a selfish move. In the end I took my mom at her word. I had to get back to Penny and the best way to do that was to go through Vietnam first. I believed we were meant to be together, so I followed my heart and chose that route.

But first there was the little matter of heading to a war.

14
BIEN HOA BLUES

ONCE AGAIN, I found myself departing McChord Air Force Base in Seattle, Washington, in March 1970, winging west over the Pacific on a chartered commercial airline. It had been two years since I left this airport for Taiwan. In some ways this trip was similar; in others it was way different.

Then I was a green, wide-eyed kid, totally clueless as to what awaited me. Now, I was older and a little more worldly at least, but I still didn't really know what I was headed into. I did grasp that it could be a rougher ride. Because of that, fear finally began to lurk. I knew it was possible things might not end well.

Soldiers from every branch of the service filled the plane, but the majority were Army guys. Peering out the plane's tiny cabin window, I occasionally caught glimpses of deep blue-gray patches of water through the clouds.

Bored expressions, restless movements and gallows humor camouflaged the anxiety of the passengers as the monotony of hours in the air weighed us all down. Likely some were merely curious about how their lives might drastically change in the coming year; others surely felt a rising tug of apprehension at being thrown into combat for the first time.

What would it be like to be shot at? Dwelling on that notion produced a strange brew of curiosity and nervousness in me. After all, most of us were either in our late teens or had just entered our 20s. And now we were on a trip to a "Twilight Zone" world of unknown foreign goblins and terrors, intent on killing us. No one said it, but we all knew for far too many of us in this plane, it could well be a 23-hour, one-way excursion.

Some guys enjoyed cracking jokes, others told war stories about Vietnam gathered from friends who had been there and returned. A few, like me, stayed quiet. I kept thinking about how lucky I was not to be going where many of these Army types were headed. Snatches of conversation informed me that a lot of them would be dropped at in-country fire bases or in helicopter squadrons.

This war did not have front lines like many do. The fighting could and did erupt anywhere. It wasn't quite as spine-chilling for those of us in the Air Force. We would be relatively safe on a guarded base, with access to barracks, beds and beer. For that comparative comfort, guys like me were dubbed REMFs—rear echelon mother fuckers.

A medium-sized Army guy with short blonde hair and glasses across the aisle from me kept busy by entertaining everyone within earshot. He was putting up a good front. It didn't hit me until later, but I'd wager he was scared shitless and the comedy show was his way to bury those qualms. He told us he was from a small town in Oklahoma.

"Ya know, I'm going to the Cav when we get there. I'll be riding shotgun on a Huey," he said, with more than a touch of pride and bravado.

Translated, he would be a door gunner, exposing himself by hanging out of the open side of a Huey helicopter, flying just above the jungles and rice paddies while he sprayed bullets toward the ground from an M-60 machine gun.

"Glad it's not me," I thought to myself.

"Yeah," he said loudly, with a chuckle. "I heard the life expectancy of a door gunner is about five minutes."

People around him sniggered a little nervously. I just looked at him. Should I tell him he was crazy or to just please shut up? The conversation did not soothe my mental well-being at all, so I picked up my book and dropped out of listening to the dialogue. Death was not a subject I wished to dwell on, especially my own.

It was near impossible to catch many Zs in the plane's seats that were clearly not built for sleeping. The only distraction other than reading was the good-looking stewardesses, as they were known back then. They all were pleasant, friendly and flirty and constantly ran back and forth waiting on us. Pity probably drove them, but some guys ignored that realistic motivation and played the Casanova role to the hilt. They knew it would be their last chance to flirt with a "round-eyed" woman for a year.

After what seemed an eternity, the fasten seat belt sign blinked on and the pilot announced our descent. Butterflies immediately took wing in my stomach. We streaked downward through wispy clouds that obscured the ground. Suddenly, MIG fighters buzzed our sinking aircraft as machine gun tracers and rockets whizzed by in the air. We were going to get shot down!

That didn't really happen, of course. It was simply the scenario my overactive imagination briefly created as we descended, as if the actual potential for death on the ground wasn't enough.

As we flew lower, the tension in the plane ramped higher. No one spoke, no one joked and most everyone was breathing shallowly. We all strained to catch a better glimpse of ground through the clouds.

When the aircraft finally broke through, we saw patches of dry red-brown clay mingled with green shoots springing out of rice fields. As we drew closer to Tan Son Nhut Air Base near Saigon, we could see small figures with conical bamboo hats bending over in the paddies or walking in lanes behind rickety-looking carts drawn by water buffalo.

Then in a loud voice, a comedian up near the front of the plane quipped, "OK, we seen it, now let's turn around and go home."

Laughter erupted throughout the cabin, a calming balm for rattled nerves.

As we walked down the steps off the plane onto the tarmac a little muddled, jittery and rumpled looking in our khakis and fatigues, an explosion of sweltering heat, heavy and humid, smacked us in the face, triggering instant sweat.

We had no idea then that this was just another typical day in the 'Nam, at least when it was dry. In this country, torrential monsoons rolled in for months at a time, rain plunging from the dark skies in curtains of unending waves, turning the incessant red dust into red mud. I quickly learned and agreed with the oft-used phrase: "It's raining like a cow pissing on a flat rock."

As we kept walking to a terminal, we passed by a loose, lounging collection of grubby-looking veterans in filthy camouflage and jungle greens waiting nearby. They would take our seats on the plane—now dubbed a Freedom Bird—for their own trip back to the World. These war zone veterans had been in "Indian

Country"—a common slang name for the battlefield that was South Vietnam—for the past year and couldn't wait to leave.

We would later learn more common local slang that identified many of these guys as the "grunts" whose main job was "humping the boonies" in the jungle, hunting for the "gooks."

Some were quietly staring at the ground or were somewhere else, off into space. But many of them, in a joyful, ritual hazing, heckled and harassed us as we trudged past in the sweltering heat.

We heard, "Hey Cherries, goooooood luck! Welcome to hell!"

The temperature felt right.

Some bragged about leaving: "Hey man, I'm so short I could parachute off a dime!"

Not to be outdone, another yelled, "Ah man, I'm so short, I get greasy balls when I walk across butter."

Being short meant your tour of duty was up or nearly over.

From another: "Alllriiiight, fresh meat for the grinder! Look at these sad sack FNGs."

FNG was short for "fucking new guy," the moniker stamped on every new arrival to Vietnam, no matter their branch of the military.

Some of us were directed to a bus for a short trip to Bien Hoa Air Base. The first thing I noticed, after the oppressive heat, humidity and harassment, was the wire mesh over all of the open bus windows.

"Hey, what's with the wire over the windows," I asked, passing the driver as I boarded the bus.

"Well that there's called your grenade stopper. Any gook tries to toss a grenade into the bus as we drive by, it'll bounce right back to 'em," he replied matter of factly. I took my seat quietly and looked out through that wire mesh with a new appreciation and apprehension about where I had ended up. Thankfully the bus trip was uneventful and not a whole lot different than my trip two years ago from Taipei to CCK, with all the attending traffic craziness and abnormal and repulsive odors.

Once I mustered in at Bien Hoa in the heart of the III Corps tactical zone located in south central South Vietnam, I was immediately enrolled in weapons training. Most of the other airmen and soldiers dispatched here had completed this firearms schooling before leaving the states. But since my route here was a little unique, being relatively nearby in Taiwan and then going home briefly on emergency leave, I had missed that training.

I was briefed on automatic handguns, the M-16 rifle and the M-60 machine gun and I fired them all at targets down range. I had to toss a grenade and fire the mortar-like, single-shot M-79 grenade launcher, which could hurl a 40mm grenade from 80-to-400 yards.

I was a decent shot and I had earned marksman ribbons previously, so I felt pretty confident. Turns out that self-assurance was overblown when it came to the M-79. The trainer showed me how to break open the sawed-off looking barrel and load a grenade before clapping it closed.

I raised the large rectangular sight, estimated the range, elevated and tucked the stock against my shoulder and pulled the trigger.

"Thunk," was the sound of the grenade as it leapt from the barrel and propelled the stock back into my right shoulder.

Turns out I wasn't so great at range estimation. The grenade arched skyward and kept going and going and going.

"Ah, shit," the trainer said, as we stared, transfixed.

It came down way too close to the safety embankment around the range. And not so far away from that explosion was a tower manned by two Army of Vietnam (ARVN) lookouts inside. "Ka-boom!" The blast scared the shit out of me, the trainer and for sure the tower guards who immediately got on their radio to squawk at my near miss.

So much for good relations with our allies. Surprisingly, I got another try, with a lot closer supervision, and managed to complete the course without killing or injuring anyone and without damaging relations with Marvin the ARVN, as our allies were sarcastically known by most of the grunts.

15
TYPING AND TESTING FATE

TRAINING COMPLETE, I was assigned to Charlie Flight, which meant I would be on the shift guarding the perimeter of the base in the dead of night. That pretty much meant every night. At best, we would get one or two days off a month.

Bien Hoa, the first base in Vietnam to be attacked back in 1964, was enclosed by concertina wire. Spaced inside the perimeter were above-ground bunkers, encircled and topped with rows of sandbags which were supposed to shield you from bullets and shrapnel.

They were nice to have but it was a small measure of comfort. On Jan. 31, 1968, just two years before I arrived, the Viet Cong attacked the base during the TET Offensive, intending to capture and take over the flight line, one of the busiest in the world. They partially succeeded in that fight, which became known as the Battle of Bien Hoa.

Hanoi launched a series of massive attacks across South Vietnam during TET—the Vietnamese New Year—designed for victory and as a catalyst to bring the already grinding war to an end. It began at 3 a.m. with well-coordinated assaults. The VC launched about 150 rockets and mortars at Bien Hoa, followed closely by two battalions of hardened Viet Cong soldiers who charged the east perimeter of the base.

MADE IN TAIWAN

The tip of the spear of the enemy's attack was focused on an old concrete French bunker. They began firing mortars and RPGs—rocket propelled grenades—on the position. Some of the VC penetrated the perimeter, but the air cops fought back furiously, keeping the majority of the foe at bay, at least for the moment.

The defenders were backed by U.S. Army Cobra gunships that swooped in, hitting the charging VC with rockets and miniguns. The Cobra's guns could fire more than 2,000 rounds per minute.

Crews and pilots for F-100 Super Saber jet fighters managed to clear explosion debris from the airstrip, allowing them to take off to conduct air strikes on the enemy hunkered down near the runway. It was possibly the only time Air Force pilots attacked their own base. All of these fierce counterattacks eventually drained the energy out of the VC's assault.

Meanwhile, commanders directed other airmen to the perimeter and units of the Army and ARVNs rolled in to reinforce the base. Then, an ARVN battalion counterattacked and drove the VC back. The assault cost our side: a dozen killed and nearly two dozen wounded. Although the enemy offensive was ultimately repelled, the TET assaults played a major role in weakening public support for the war back home.

Since that time, the VC had regularly dropped mortars and RPGs within the confines of Bien Hoa, but they had not attempted another ground assault—yet. There was no way to predict if or when sappers might test our perimeter again. If they did, it was highly likely I would have a front-row seat to all of those hostilities as a first line of defense.

TYPING AND TESTING FATE

Contemplating these scenarios made me remember the full-of-bluster, immodest Army guy on the in-bound plane who laughed about his short life expectancy as a Huey door-gunner. Seemed I might be sitting right next to him.

These comforting deliberations were bouncing around in my head when S.Sgt. Lucas Sullivan entered my small barracks living space a couple of days before I would head for the outer ring of fences.

"Hey Sgt. Brown, how ya doing?

Welcome to 'Nam," he said, smiling. "You gettin' adjusted?"

"Yeah, a little bit. Still trying to figure out where everything is."

"You'll get there. The base layout is pretty simple and most of the natives are friendly, inside the gates," he said, laughing.

"Huh, yeah. I've been around a bit and some guys have been helpful. What's up? Do you need something from me?"

"Yeah maybe. I was going over your records and I have a question. Can you type?" he asked.

By now, I had been in the military long enough to gain some wisdom. And one insight that ranked at the top was to never volunteer information about yourself until you knew why they wanted it.

"Well, maybe. Why do you wanna know?"

Sullivan gave a knowing smirk.

"We need someone to work in a small intelligence unit. You'd work off base in an underground tactical operations center bunker with the Army, the ARVNs and the Popular Forces local militia.

"Basically you'll be base liaison for the intel gathered in this region. If the base is attacked, you'll feed us real time information to help coordinate a response. And every day you'll take all the intel for that day and compile it into a daily report."

Hmm, I thought, this sure sounds a heck of a lot better than trying to stay awake all night in a perimeter bunker, hoping to avoid getting my throat cut by an enemy sapper.

"What kind of shifts would I have to work?" I asked.

"Ah, that's the best part," Sullivan responded. "You work two 12-hour overnights, get 24 hours off, then two 12-hour day shifts followed by 48 hours off."

He didn't have to ask me again if I was interested.

"Yup, I can type," I said, presenting my widest grin.

And so I dodged all-night guard duty on a chancy fence line and started my new job, thanks to my high school typing class. I was full-on REMF—although I might argue it was dangerous to leave the security of the base every day to drive through town to get to work—but it was clear within a couple of shifts I had made the right choice. The assignment was as advertised and I worked with some fun, crazy and fascinating people.

I was the sole Air Force guy in the command post. Sullivan or another airman would pick me up in a jeep and take me off base to the nearby III Corps Compound and the underground TOC—tactical operation center.

Most times it was slow-moving work, unless the VC unleashed a rocket attack or the militia forces spotted enemy movement. Then we would erupt into a whirlwind of activity as we coordinated information amongst our counterparts and shared real-time results with our respective people—in my case, the air base. In some ways, like crafting police incident reports,

TYPING AND TESTING FATE

this was another precursor to my future. A decade later I would also be filing critical accounts to inform people, only as a newspaper journalist.

If I didn't mind walking on the crazy side, and I didn't, this intel job offered some unexpected benefits. Our operation was connected to a helicopter squadron with missions of reconnaissance and support in the III Corps area.

During the day, the choppers would fly out to remote artillery fire bases, bringing mail and supplies, like rations, water and other essentials the troops needed out in the boonies. These fire bases were isolated in the middle of hostile country with the important mission of supporting infantry operations. They were filled with a battery of artillery and surrounded by earthen berms, barbed wire and Claymore mines.

It probably wasn't intentional, but whenever I did tag along for a ride it seemed like the base would fire off a 105mm howitzer for what I deemed was way too close to our chopper as we flew in or departed. The resulting "ka-boom" was a body slam that always scared the crap out of me.

At night, our Hueys along with a Cobra gunship flew missions known as "Firefly." These were hunter-killer operations designed to attack ground targets while flying just above the jungle treetops. Because of where I worked, I was allowed to "ride along" on these operations, too.

These jaunts added another whole level of adventure to my Vietnam experiences. I didn't spend any time contemplating just how wrong things could easily go. I was young and still felt at least somewhat invincible. I eventually earned more than a dozen flying hours.

It was foolish and ill-advised behavior on so many levels, emphasis on ill-advised. I had no real role, I was simply a passenger. So usually I did not get a headset that allowed the crew to converse with one another. Not sure why I never asked. Mistake No. 1.

Because I didn't know what the hell I was doing and because I felt unneeded, extra cargo along for a ride, the first couple of times I went up I didn't want to bother the crew by asking how to strap myself in properly within the harnesses and seat belts. Apparently I still harbored that childhood foundational lesson of not being a bother to people, but I'm pretty sure my parents would have considered and welcomed this as an exception had I been wise enough to ask. That reluctance to ask a reasonable question left my continued good health relying on how tight a grip I managed to keep on the bird's interior structure. Basically I was improperly strapped, shaky and stupid in a flying machine with its door wide open, zipping along hundreds of feet in the air. Mistake No. 2.

Once and only once I chose to ride along on a day time resupply mission after a night downing way more beers than necessary and getting very little sleep. My head ached and drummed repetitively; my stomach flopped like a fish out of water, but I thought the fresh air might clear my senses. Ha! Big Mistake No. 3.

Per usual and as a passenger, I didn't get a headset that connected me to the crew's communication link. It was only later I figured out someone had detected and shared my unsteady condition with the pilots. All was good as we flew along nice and level and I was enjoying the air blowing on my face.

Then the Huey dropped nearly straight down, like a giant had lassoed the bird and was pulling it to earth. I swear my stomach pushed up through my brain. With a white-knuckle death grasp, I held onto the rim of my seat. The pilot then raised the chopper's tail in the air and shot up and forward.

"This is how I'm going to die in Vietnam," I thought, suddenly terrified.

The chopper pitched to the left so I had a view and a way-too-easy exit out of the side door. The pilot then pitched the bird over to the right so I was looking at blue sky and cottony clouds.

I didn't know what the hell was going on and my face had to be frozen in wide-eyed panic. I turned to my right and looked at the co-pilot who was looking back at me and grinning.

He motioned for me to grab a headset. Nervous about letting go of the seat, I fumbled for an unhooked one and put it over my ears. "You alright back there," he asked, still grinning.

I managed a sick, weak smile.

"Ah, I guess. What's going on? We in trouble?"

"Nah, we're good. We were practicing a little down and out. You know, a little dipsy-doodle. All's good. Back to normal so hang in there."

Somehow I managed to keep the contents of my stomach from painting the chopper's cabin. After this big blunder, I passed on boarding any flights after a night of over imbibing.

As exciting as the resupply missions were, they were nothing compared to riding along on the bold, nighttime Firefly operation. When the Army lieutenant I worked with explained how it worked, I had to go see for myself.

I was in a war zone but had a relatively safe job where, but for a few brief times during a month, I spent my free time reading novels. Not really much to brag about there and I was also a little bored. But going on a Firefly was a way to inject some excitement and maybe secure a war story or two of my own.

The missions offered drama, potential danger and an extraordinary, exceptional thrill. Obviously, I didn't think very deeply about this; I just climbed aboard.

A Firefly operation involved several helicopters. The first was a Huey, known as the "light ship." The second, an AH-1 Cobra, was the gunship. Both were given directions from a command and control chopper. One night I scrambled aboard the Huey, ducking under the already twirling rotor blades, which was more of an instinctive action than a need.

I settled in a seat against the interior wall and looked at a cluster of landing lights taken from a C-130 cargo aircraft and mounted next to the door gunner's machine gun to the right and pointed out of the side of the aircraft. The lights were powerful enough to light up large sections of nighttime jungle, depending on the height of the light ship.

The pilot powered up, the tail lifted and we were airborne, followed by the Cobra. Soon, at 1,000 or more feet, we were flying over the jungle, directed by the command and control helicopter to a region where nothing should have been moving on the ground after a certain time at night. That area was known as a "free-fire zone."

The pilot eventually slowed, hovered briefly and then began a rapid spiraling, nose-to-the-ground descent toward the jungle, enveloped in darkness. The Cobra ship stayed high above us. Waves of a musty, dank smell washed through the interior of the helicopter, reeking of soil dampness and rotting vegetation.

It was an unexpected, chilling stench that grounded me and woke me up to the kind of danger I had willingly enrolled myself in. That dulled some of the exhilaration and awe. Suddenly this wasn't so harmless. The Huey pilot skimmed across treetops, imitating the little beetle it was named after by alternately switching the helicopter's lights on and off, searching for ground targets. These risky missions were designed to surprise or interrupt enemy troops, so at times the bird flew dark, which upped the potential for disaster exponentially, flying that close to the ground.

Anything or anyone moving in this "no man's land" would be fair game for the hell the Cobra gunship would unleash from above us. Depending on the terrain, the pilot mixed our height and speed from a couple hundred feet to 20 feet above the trees, often flying low and slow or even at times simply hovering. It was complicated and required some nifty piloting as the guy at the helm altered air speed and height and had to focus and adjust his vision between the blazing light and the surrounding darkness.

These tree-top maneuvers practically begged an RPG-toting VC hiding in the brush below to try to bring down this fat, inviting and exposed target. And they did try. Mistake No. 4—I'm sitting in the "light ship".

While our bird appeared as sacrificial bait, anyone bold enough to try to shoot at us from the ground opened themselves up to a lethal nightmare from above. The Cobra was the first-ever dedicated attack helicopter and it was loaded with rockets, a minigun and a grenade launcher. Literally, it was a flying killing machine and about the third time I went out on a Firefly mission I saw it in action.

Our Huey pilot was sliding us around turns above the jungle, searchlights occasionally exploding the inky dark with sun-like bursts of light on the ground below.

As we flew over a section of jungle, the crew spotted movement between some trees and thick brush. We swung around again and there it was, someone or something moving quickly through the jungle.

Our pilot launched into action, making the call and perfecting a hasty down-and-out airborne maneuver, immediately clearing us from that air space. The Cobra swooped in behind, dropping quickly in a steep descent. In moments it hurled mind-blowing firepower toward the ground, sending a couple of rocket salvos into the area.

"Whoosh, whoosh," and two rockets shot out of their pods, flames lighting up their tails with smoke trails arching to the ground.

On impact, the noise of two roaring explosions and clouds of smoke mushroomed upward and at least one large tree toppled to the ground.

The Cobra swung back again, slowed to a hover and then unleashed its minigun with torrents of 7.62 mm rounds.

"Zzzzzzzziiiiiiiitttttttttt, zzzzzzzziiiiiiiitttttttttt, zzzzzzzz-ziiiiiiiitttttttttt, zzzzzzzziiiiiiiitttttttttt." Long streaming tails of red tracers linked the mini gun's rotating barrel and the ground, skipping crazily around the area where we had spotted movement.

The minigun sounded like a swarm of angry giant bees or an out-of-control jackhammer running at a super-fast speed. This swift and lethal action with an ability to produce massive destruction took my breath away. I'd never seen anything like it. Whatever had been moving down there surely was no longer doing so.

I flew on a couple of these missions. It wasn't required and had my superiors back on base known about this unsanctioned

TYPING AND TESTING FATE

flying, I likely would have been ordered to stay grounded. But I took wing, at least in small part, because I harbored some guilt knowing the kind of war the grunts and ground pounders dealt with, humping those jungles every night and day. Comparatively, I was relatively comfortable as a REMF.

One night when I got to work at the operations bunker I was told that the night before a VC had fired an RPG at the Firefly, narrowly missing the bird.

That was enough for me. I made the unilateral command decision that my feet would remain planted firmly on the ground until I boarded a Freedom Bird that signaled the end of my Vietnam tour.

16
REMF NO LONGER

THE ARMY AND MARINES made up the majority of the jungle rats who were plunged deeply into the boonies in the down-and-dirty fight of this war. They spent their time in country on constant patrol. They often worked under triple canopy darkness, trudging through treacherous terrain, boot-sucking mud and the ever-present moisture of impenetrable vegetation.

They patrolled, walking in ponchos that offered minimal protection from the relentless, pounding monsoon rains, shivering in the cold that briefly followed. When it wasn't raining during the day, jungle fatigues sopped up buckets of body sweat produced by the sweltering, oppressive heat and humidity of the tropics.

Not all of the enemy walked on two legs. Swarms of vicious, hungry mosquitos, torrents of nasty, aggressive red ants, skittering poisonous scorpions, four-foot long centipedes and enormous venomous snakes also took offense at having their homes invaded by Americans. They defended their territory.

The grunts constantly dealt with waves of fatigue, fear and monotony along with the 80-pounds or more of weapons, ammo and other equipment they packed and humped into the jungles. Uncertainty and the stress of hypervigilance were constant companions as they tried to stay alert for daytime ambushes, nighttime perimeter attacks or treacherous boobytraps that could take a limb or a life.

They were rugged and deserved all respect for facing this stress and trauma day after day. There was a coping, shrug-the-shoulders adage used widely by the troops in Vietnam meant to brush off everything from the stupid to FUBAR-level bad that would occur regularly: "It don't mean nothin'!"

That was a refrain that helped us get through to the next disagreeable thing.

I didn't have to deal with any of that extremely dangerous mess, including the endless fear of walking into instant death around the next tree from an enemy ambush or booby trap. But there were occasional bursts of chaos and fear that snapped our boredom. While I was at Bien Hoa, neither the VC or NVA tried to overrun the base like they did during Tet 1968. It wasn't a total pass, however.

During my eight months in country they hit us just under a dozen times with a variety of rocket and mortar assaults that caused death, injury and ruin. The first attack I experienced came within days of my arrival. The VC fired three 107mm rockets just before 10 a.m., which thankfully impacted just off base, with no damage or casualties. But the surreal assault sparked in me a somber reality—for the first time in my life someone wanted to kill me. Damn.

They tried again, several times. With a couple of exceptions, the enemy used the cover of predawn darkness to launch missiles. That timing gave us a minor advantage. Guard towers 40 feet high and ringed with sandbags were scattered around the base and manned by either Americans or ARVNs.

REMF NO LONGER

When the VC launched rockets or mortars, the lookouts could see the initial flash of the projectiles in the distance in the dark. The sentries then scrambled to set off a base-wide warning siren, which was loud enough to roust anyone from sweet dreams of home and round-eyed girls.

When the siren shrieked, we were supposed to run out of our hootches to the nearest bunker. There wasn't much time. You could often hear explosions impact before you got inside the bunker.

Those detonations always provided an extra goose. Ironically the bunker dash, often run in bare feet, caused more injuries than the falling shells. The bunkers weren't far, but a mad scramble of dozens of men in the dark all trying to dive through a shelter's small entranceway led to bumps, bruises and a few breaks.

After a time, I embraced the rash lead of many guys who had already racked up some time in country. Hear the siren, roll off the bunk, crawl underneath. The move offered little protection for a direct hit, but waist-high sandbags surrounded each of our hootches, so a close hit, if not in the wrong spot, could be endured with at least some security.

The old adage that timing is everything couldn't have been truer for me in the beginning of May, when the enemy hammered us with mortars and rockets over a 28-hour period.

During those assaults, a Vietnamese civilian was killed and nearly 50 Americans and one civilian were wounded. Had I been delayed by about five minutes from getting off work that day, I would have joined that list of injured or the even more frightening list of KIA—those killed in action.

"Hey, Sully, how ya doing?" I asked as Sullivan pulled up in a jeep a little before 6 p.m. in front of the underground bunker with my relief. He was also my ride back to base. "Can you drop me at church? Going to try to make Sunday Mass."

"Sure, wherever you want to go," he said.

After my first six months in Taiwan, I had drifted away from my consistent Catholic childhood church-going days. Of course I harbored guilt about my religious desertion, but not enough to drive me back. That is, until I landed in Vietnam. Funny how a little time in a war zone can reignite your faith.

As Sully drove us onto the base, we steered toward the chapel. During the trip, we stopped at an intersection near the church before turning right. He pulled up in front of the building and I got out.

"Thanks man, see you tomorrow," I said, waving and trotting inside.

I was running a bit late and Mass had already begun. I found a space in a pew and slid in. The priest had finished the Kyrie song when an explosion tore through the air, sounding way too close to the pew I occupied.

"Get down, get down," the priest yelled.

He didn't have to say that twice. Myself and everyone around me dropped and did our best to skootch over the kneeler and under the benches. The base siren, a little late, began to wail as six more explosives slammed into the ground inside the perimeter.

That was it for that attack, thankfully, but the real scare for me was just around the corner, literally. Mass had come to an erupt end, so I started walking back to my hootch. I could see medics converging on the nearby mess hall, which had taken a direct hit, right at prime-time dinner hour.

Because there was no early warning from the towers, no one had time to take cover in a bunker. The assault began in the light of day, so the tower guards couldn't see the telltale flashes from the rockets. They hit the alarms only after the explosions began to detonate.

I was half a block from the intersection where we had stopped in the jeep earlier when I saw water gushing from a large hole in the ground. One of the seven 122mm rockets had hit the corner of the juncture, 10-feet away from where I had been sitting in the open-air jeep mere minutes before. Had we been running a little later, both Sullivan and I could have been killed or at a minimum seriously wounded.

I stood and stared at that gushing hole, unable to take my eyes off of it or my mind off the fact that fate and providence had helped me dodge a sure disaster. I was dazed the rest of the night, and when I lay down the shock of coming that close to death kept me awake for hours. I was in a shaky fugue for days after but then later, of course, it became my war story. Thankfully, it was the best one I ever had.

"Man, we stopped at this intersection and five minutes later a VC rocket hit right where we stopped. If I had gotten off work just a few minutes later, I'd be dead."

We were all lucky we didn't lose more people on that day. Over the entire 28 hours, the enemy fired 15 122mm rockets and six 82mm mortars beginning just after 1:30 a.m. Sunday on May 3 and ending at 6 a.m. the next day.

The attacks generated major havoc. The blasts took out a chopper, half of the chow hall and five vehicles. They damaged the runway, the headquarters and personnel building, blew up an aircraft petroleum and oil cart and that water main. The enemy hit the base a few more times before I left, but no attack reached the level of that May mayhem.

17

GETTING BOMBED PART II

WHILE THE VC did pound us from time to time, more often than not we damaged ourselves with a different kind of pounding—cheap beer. Hammering headaches induced by too many cans consumed triggered those self-inflicted wounds. A recurring challenge amidst the evening's entertainment was for us to stack those empty beer cans as close to the ceiling as we could get. Think of it as an adult pioneer version of Jenga.

Then we'd stand behind the container pyramid like big game hunters showing off a prize kill. Pictures from that long-ago time show us in different poses behind and around the cans, some of us shirtless with our arms around one another, often flashing a sneer or a one-finger salute aimed at the photographer. The gestures pretty much summed up how we felt about the war, Vietnam and the military in general.

One of our pet phrases when we pushed the envelope by doing something that could lead us into trouble went like this: "What are they gonna do, send me to Vietnam?"

Many guys, including myself, experienced some measure of patriotism in coming here. But after a couple of weeks of indoctrination and getting the feel of the place, most of us came to one conclusion—us being here (and by us I mean America) was bullshit. Our nation seemed to be mired in mud, accomplishing who knows what? On top of that, the vibe from some of the Vietnamese we encountered was not all that positive, and those were the guys and gals who were supposedly on our side. It certainly was a far cry from the friendship I had felt from many of the Chinese I met in Taiwan. So to say there was a little attitude going on would be an understatement.

In those days the guys who turned to alcohol for fun and to relieve mental stress were called "juicers." Many of them were higher-ranked non-commissioned officers and career military types known as "lifers."

The "heads" were the dudes firing up joints or smoking hash or getting high with other illegal substances to find that escape-our-surroundings buzz, and there was plenty of that happening.

For the most part, the heads did not respect the juicers and vice versa. At that time I was squarely in the drinking camp. Some friends smoked pot and it was easy enough to find, but I said no whenever it was offered.

Enough of that law abiding, uptight but good youngster still resided within, so I kept my distance from illicit drugs. I was curious but not yet curious enough to try a taste. Marijuana was also illegal and I had qualms about breaking the law with an illegal substance and then getting caught. That sure changed big time later, but for now I turned down several opportunities, still in fear of what it might do to me. PBR—Pabst Blue Ribbon—and Budweiser beer were my drugs of choice in Vietnam.

When I wasn't working, the base didn't offer much else in the way of entertainment. You could catch a movie, read or write letters home, but beyond those diversions the menu was thin as time continued to move slowly.

GETTING BOMBED PART II

A couple times the base sponsored a concert with a local Vietnamese band doing its best to imitate American artists of the day, playing their rock 'n roll and soul song hits. They usually weren't great musicians or vocalists and they struggled to correctly sing some of the consonant sounds, but the more you drank the better they sounded, a joke you will still hear from American music groups even today.

So most nights we entertained ourselves with stories. Our hooch housed some real clowns and storytellers. "Country Willie," aka Sgt. Clayton William, quickly became a barracks celebrity. He had wavy dark hair, whipped in curls over his forehead above bushy black brows and a left eye that tended to drift.

Through and through, he was a good old boy from Tennessee and the most colorful of a lively lot. He was the go-to guy who captured center stage and the spotlight nightly.

To regale us with tales of his audacious adventures, Country Willie would straddle the back of a chair while we gathered and sat in a semi-circle around him. As he began each saga, real or imagined, Vietnam's omnipresent sweat rolled over his brow. He'd grin impishly, close his eyes, tilt his head and begin an epic tale.

Willie loved to belt out the tunes, too. He'd grab a small mic wired into an amplified cassette player at the table by his side, lean forward over the back of the chair and serenade the room in his almost-in-key version of the day's popular songs, such as "Patches," "Stand by Your Man" or "The Fightin' Side of Me."

To accent the warbling, he'd jump up and strut jerkily across the floor. It was a little bizarre, and we couldn't tell if he was dancing or getting zapped with electric shocks. Regardless, it was entertaining and funny as hell as he mostly managed to keep the beat. It's pretty clear that an ever-present can of Budweiser in his right hand energized the performances.

The amusement would often begin after an awesome meal of steak or burgers cooked up on a homemade grill, a sawed-in-half, 50-gallon drum. Who needed the unsightly, creamy mess of shit-on-a-shingle in the mess hall?

We didn't because we had shrewd S.Sgt. Doug Duncan as a hootch mate. He had some kind of important cop function that involved operational inspections on the base, so he was well connected to guys in charge of base supplies. He constantly bartered and scrounged on our behalf to snatch up the best food and beverages.

I have no clue what he did for them in return, but we managed to live large considering our circumstances and compared to the troops around us. We were high-on-the-hog REMFs!

Frequently after an all-night shift, I trekked to the NCO club in the early morning for eggs and beer. Yep, eggs and beer. When some of the guys first told me about that combo, it sounded kind of revolting. Then I tried it. Hard to believe that beer could be better than bacon.

The alcohol—10 cents a can for PBR—worked like a liquid sleeping pill, a good thing because it was never easy to grab shut eye during the day. It was always blistering hot in Vietnam and without air conditioning the hooch was as muggy as a sauna.

The walls had slatted wooden sides and screens so a breeze might flow in, even if that air was more like an oppressive blanket than soothing or cooling. The alcohol helped put me out for a while, but any manner of racket could and did break through the brew-induced hazy dreams. And there was commotion. On more than one occasion I was "dapped" right out of a deep sleep.

GETTING BOMBED PART II

Our hooch sat close to a confluence of walkways that was an active thoroughfare. Most times folks would simply pass one another, maybe stop for a brief hello if acquainted, and then move on.

But when several soul brothers converged at those crossroads, the greeting was much more structured, formal, defined and loudly expressed. It was a time when Black guys greeted each other with a solidarity handshake known as the Dap. Actually, calling the gesticulating greeting a handshake does not do it justice.

Black soldiers stationed in the Pacific in the late 1960s during Vietnam created the salutation. Reflecting "dignity and pride," the shake became an emblem expressed by these Americans to demonstrate their commitment to their culture and to one another.

The greeting was meant to display strength, boldness and even resistance at a time of severe racial unrest back home. In the coming year, I would personally witness and be a part of that turbulence as it became more widespread within the military, too, proving, I guess, that the more things change the more they stay the same.

While different versions existed, the Dap had a configuration that changed and grew with time. What I remember then was that two guys might start by clasping hands, hooking thumbs and pulling away.

Then each person would slap palms, top-to-bottom, followed by back-of-the-hand and then front-of-the-hand sideways claps. Both guys would then raise their arms for a high-five smack.

Somewhere along the progression fingers would snap and fists would bump before the greeting came to a close—for those two guys. Etiquette required each person to greet everyone in a group in the same way, so it could get noisy and drawn out if a lot of guys hit the intersection at the same time.

The animated salutations, conducted not so far away from my bunk, jarred me out of sleep more than once with, "slap, slap, slap, slap, snap, snap, thump, thump, bump, bump, slap."

And this would go on for five minutes!

I knew it was serious business for the brothers and it was cool enough that I wanted to learn it, so a couple of my Black buddies taught me. But in the heat of the day on little rest, these salutes could also be irritating because it was harder than hell to get back to sleep in that steaming hootch.

In September, I took my week-long R&R to Taiwan so I could spend time with Penny. I was so excited and happy to see her again, but it was a whirlwind visit. She came up to Taipei to meet me and we spent the week hanging out and sightseeing around the area.

For me, it felt like I landed for a day and then had to turn around and get back on the plane for Vietnam. We had stayed in touch a few times a month through letters, but the contact wasn't that satisfying and I worried about her. I knew she had gone back to work and I didn't like that much, but she assured me all was well.

Had I been more observant while on leave, I might have noticed some changes in her since I had left Taiwan. On my visit we still talked about and planned our future together. But I still didn't know if I would be coming back here when my Vietnam tour was finished in February. The Air Force hadn't issued any orders for a new assignment.

Penny talked a good game during my brief visit, but looking back I think she might have believed my pledge to return was still an empty promise. She had seen it before, probably many times, through the experiences of her girlfriends who had been left behind, promises unfulfilled from their American boyfriends.

But she didn't express doubts and I was too in love and clueless to pick up on any signs, if there were any. I was so determined I would get back to her, one way or another, even if I was sent back to the U.S. first. But I wanted to believe things were fine and that it would all work out, so I adopted a feeling of confidence that all would be well. It gave me some relief, but those sentiments were premature, as it turned out.

Soon after I returned to Bien Hoa, I hatched what I thought would be a sure-fire way to get the Air Force to send me back to CCK and Penny. That was the upside, but it would require me to sacrifice some freedom. Once back, I told the military I would re-enlist, provided they cut me orders for Taiwan when my tour ended in Vietnam.

By then, I had been in the Air Force for more than two-and-a-half years. By re-enlisting I would essentially be starting all over again, with credit for time served. But I would also receive a financial bonus, which would help pay for our wedding costs. The strategy worked even better than I hoped.

I reupped on November 3 and got my tour in 'Nam shortened by three months. Less than two weeks later, with four more years ahead of me in the Air Force, I was winging my way back to CCK and the love of my life—or so I believed.

18
TERRIBLE TUMBLES

I HAD HOPED to get reassigned back onto Town Patrol when I returned to CCK but no such luck. At least they didn't throw me back out onto the flight line where I would be required to spend night and day humping aircraft.

Instead I was assigned to law enforcement on the base, so I was either riding patrol doing real police work or crewing the Main Gate, where we had to check everyone's ID before they entered the base. At night that duty was often a chore because each CCK Smoker returned packed mostly with half-to-fully inebriated Americans.

Because of my work schedule and training sessions, I spent a lot of time those first couple of weeks on the base when I first arrived. Whenever I could, I hopped the bus and traveled to town to see Penny at the bar where she worked.

Any overnight stay was rare, in part because of my schedule and because she said she was letting a girlfriend, who didn't have a place, crash at her apartment. I hated hanging out with her at work but for the moment it was mostly the only way to see her.

In my mind, especially after Vietnam, we were apart way too many hours and these were always times of inner turmoil for me. I wondered and worried where she was, what she was doing and who she was doing it with or who was coming to the bar to see her. Flirting with American servicemen, after all, was her job. I wanted her to quit but she wanted to keep earning money.

"I make extra money for us," she would say.

I wanted to believe her but my instinct, which I was learning to trust, suggested something darker.

I still had friends on Town Patrol and I hadn't been back at CCK all that long when one of my cop buddies working downtown dropped a dime on her. He said he had noticed during bar checks that she was often talking to one American guy in particular. He had even spotted them walking closely together down the street.

These stories kicked me squarely in the gut. I wanted to think he was mistaken but my heart whispered the distressing message of impending treachery. If it was true, she had been lying to me and probably still would continue to lie. I needed to find out for myself.

On a night that Penny expected me to work, I made my way downtown. I had convinced my cop friend to cruise through her bar a couple of times and let me know if anything was going on. He brought back the miserable news that she seemed to be enjoying herself with this mystery friend. The stage was set; I just had to give it some time.

I hung out in one of the other bars in misery. Much later after I knew she was off work, I walked up to her apartment. And there I was, in the midst of a progressing nightmare, standing in front of her door. Oh, did I mention I had been drinking all evening? Yeah. I pounded on and kicked that door. And when she opened it my worst fear turned to reality right in front of me. She was with another man.

TERRIBLE TUMBLES

I snapped, but the anguish of the situation overwhelmed the anger of the moment. The fury would come later, but in that instant my legs were taken out from under me. That was a good thing; it kept anyone from getting hurt, me included. She was together with him and it couldn't be clearer they were lovers. Simple as that. I was crushed. I'll never forget that devastating sight. I walked away, humiliated and shattered. The curtain had collapsed on my great love affair. Despair descended over me like a dark shroud.

Recovery was a protracted process. There were times I wondered if I ever fully recovered. Like any good wine I've improved over the ensuing decades, but developing and maintaining trust and the fear of commitment have long been issues for me and they can certainly be traced back to this wretched deception.

My still-young naïve brain of that time could not comprehend how this ostensible loving bond with the potential for a bright future of a life ahead could dissolve so easily, so quickly and so cruelly. Obviously, I had forgotten what I did to my high school girlfriend, Rebecca, in my very first days in Taiwan.

Like many people, I had erected some defensive walls around my emotions as I grew up, but this vile experience stimulated me to build them even thicker and raise them higher as a shield against more intense pain and fear. I didn't do this consciously, but over time I became more wary around people, especially romantic partners. I was self-protecting my emotions as I waited for the sure-to-come disaster.

This personal defense became the way I lived my life, never quite trusting, always alert for trouble or deceit, and that colored many of my future relationships with women. I wondered if I would ever fully trust a member of the opposite sex again.

Immediately after this shock of a lifetime I existed in a dark funk for months. I sought escape and release, so I turned to alcohol and, for the first time in my life, marijuana.

Just before all of this personal trauma occurred, my roommate on base, a fellow police officer whose name I can no longer remember—no surprise considering the activities we shared—had called me over to the closet in our room.

"TC, c'mere, I want to show you something," he said.

I ambled over.

"Take a look at this," he said as he opened the top of his full-to-the-brim, long green duffle bag.

I leaned over to look inside and inhaled the heavy-duty aroma that an oversize sack full of pot generates.

"Holy shit," I said as he laughed.

He urged me to fire up a joint with him then, but I said no thanks. That refusal changed quickly after a cheating fiancée blew out my stability.

In those days, marijuana flowed into CCK like beer flowing freely out of an open tap on a 15-gallon keg. Our home-based C-130 cargo planes flew essential daily missions that supported operations during Vietnam, hopscotching people and supplies around several countries in Asia. While their operations often went without a hitch, they also could be dangerous, especially when flying into "hot" zones in Vietnam that came under enemy fire. These heroic air crews put their lives on the line every day to complete these critical sorties. But when some of the planes returned to Taiwan, they weren't empty when it came to contraband, like enemy flags, helmets, knives, bayonets and of course, pot. Some of these birds were stocked with large volumes of cannabis, which was plentiful and easy to buy in Vietnam or Thailand, for a lucrative return trip to Taiwan.

The base security police worked customs, checking returning aircraft for prohibited material. Of course not every aircraft crew member dealt in contraband, and many of the cops were tough cookies who diligently searched those aircraft. But some did practice the black art of black marketing and some of the cops didn't check these incoming birds too closely, if you know what I mean.

Somehow the two factions would find each other and the crew would reward those casual aircraft inspections with skim off the top. So finding marijuana to smoke at CCK, even when you were a policeman, was not problematic. Weed was cheap and plentiful.

I was a nervous, uncertain pot smoker at first. The stuff was strong and I was concerned it would mentally drop me off the deep end and I might not be able to make my way back to reality. The first time I toked, I inhaled so little that nothing happened.

"Eh, this isn't doing much for me," I confessed to my roomie.

The next couple of times he fired up a doobie, I begged off. But he was persistent so I circled back and tried it again. Each time I was a little less tentative and soon enough I began to catch a pleasant buzz. And I liked it.

It helped me blot out the sorrow that seasoned my moods after my face-off with Penny. We smoked right in our barracks room, but first we would fold a towel and jam it into the bottom of the door jamb to keep any telltale smoke or scent from leaking out.

After seeing it everywhere for the previous couple of years, I had finally stepped into the land of the "head." More and more guys seemed to be doing drugs and not just pot, but I didn't jump in with both feet. I still kept a foot in the "juicer" world. I drank to drown my mourning and in the process damn near drowned myself.

It was stupid; I was stupid. My actions were so brainless I came close to breaking my neck, literally, and seriously hurting two other people in the process, none of it purposefully.

Gina was one of Penny's best Chinese friends and she and I were close enough that I felt she was one person I could commiserate with. It was probably obvious to Gina, but by talking to her about this situation, I was hoping my misery and sorrow would be relayed back to Penny. I knew it was a long shot, but maybe after hearing about all the pain I was in she would have second thoughts about this other guy and we might find a way to reconnect. I understood any reunion based on my sad-sack tale would be motivated by pity, but as dejected as I was, I'd take it. I was desperate.

As I poured out my tale of woe in a bar, Gina was sweet enough to listen. But one night it all really came crashing down in reality. I'm unsure about the amount of alcohol I consumed that evening, but let's say it was prodigious. I was as smashed as I had ever been without passing out. Losing consciousness would have made for a better outcome, but not much of a story.

I was struggling to coordinate my movements well enough so I could simply get off the bar stool without falling, but a bigger unanticipated challenge lay ahead. To get out of the bar I would have to maneuver down a flight of 20-or-more steep steps to the ground level. Gina was smart enough and kind enough to know I desperately needed help.

TERRIBLE TUMBLES

"Betty, come here. Help me take outside," she yelled, recruiting a coworker.

Betty walked over as I hung onto the bar, swaying. We staggered and rocked our way toward the stairway. With arms wrapped around their necks, I was hanging onto the ladies like they were life preservers keeping me on my feet—and they were, literally.

These were two tiny Asian girls trying to support a 170-pound, 5-foot, 9-inch very drunk man. We made it to the top of the staircase and even through my blurry vision it looked like we were peering down from the top of a mountain peak.

"OK, lessss go," I slurred.

I took one tentative step, then another, hanging most of my weight on the shoulders of my diminutive escorts. When I extended my right foot toward the third step, it moved. Or at least in my muddled mind it did.

Somehow I missed that stair entirely and immediately the three of us were airborne and plummeting downward. I remember bodies rolling over me and me rolling over bodies on the way down. The women screamed and hollered the entire way. I probably did, too. We finally came to a stop, limbs tangled, at the bottom landing.

"Oh, oh, ah, uhhh," we all moaned.

I lay for a moment, trying to figure out if I had broken something. But shockingly all my extremities seemed to be in working order. "Gina, Betty, you OK? Can you move?" I mumbled as I crawled up to my hands and knees.

Both young ladies, dazed, pushed themselves up slowly to a sitting position. They looked at one another and then me. They rattled Chinese back and forth as employees and customers rushed downstairs to see if we needed medical attention or a coroner.

"Yes, we OK," Gina said.

Someone ran down the street to alert the cops on Town Patrol, who showed up to check on the commotion. Miraculously, with the exception of bruising, none of us were seriously injured.

I've often heard that if and when you take a fall, you should relax to avoid harm. I'm still unsure how the girls were unscathed in that terrible tumble. Had to be a miracle. For me? I'm surmising the quantity of alcohol in my system put me in a rag-doll-relaxed state and that saved my dumb ass.

That episode could have ended way differently, with serious injuries or even a death. It really was a very long way down to the bottom. For most people that horrible fall would set off loud alarms. It would have been a wake-up call.

For me, not so much. Without realizing it at the time, that mighty spill symbolized my own soon-to-come principled downfall. Obviously some of my past behavior hadn't exactly been stellar, but the damage was more self-inflicted.

Now I was about to commit a crime against a person.

19
REVENGE, THE BITTER FRUIT

I CONTINUED TO WALLOW in wretchedness and commit stupid acts. In the wee hours of one early morning, after an evening of overindulgence, I decided it was a good idea to find Penny's family and appeal my case to them. Forget the fact they didn't speak much English and I didn't speak Chinese. I'd find a way to get my message across.

I took a taxi to their neighborhood, stumbled to a doorway and knocked on the door to plead my case. There was one minor problem. I had the wrong house. So, I only managed to piss off the confused Chinese family that hesitantly opened the door, embarrassing myself in the process. Definitely not a step in the right direction for improving cross-cultural relations.

I continued to feel lost in more than a few ways. It was hard to concentrate and I'm sure I bothered everyone around me with my despair. I was hurt, I was sad and I was angry. Then one friend came up with an idea to relieve the pain for at least one of those emotions.

Brent Lincoln was a robust, hail-fellow-well-met security policeman with dark eyes and short wavy black hair. He was often my patrol partner and we had become close friends. He was married to a Chinese woman and they had two young children, so the family kind of took pity on me, the poor waif who had lost his love and his way.

One night as we sat on his porch after we had plowed through steaks, a few Budweisers and my Penny melancholy, Brent got a notion.

"Ya know, TC, I got an idea. We know who this guy is. We know where to find his military records. What if one night we decided to swing by and take a little peek at those records?"

Because we were the on-base police, we had master keys to all of the administration buildings.

"OK, so we look at his records and then what? Are you hoping to find some dirt?" I asked.

"No, but maybe we cause this asshole some of the pain he's put you through," he said.

My next thought would not be one I would enter on an application for sainthood, but I perked up and a little-too-eagerly asked, "What have you got in mind?"

And that's how in the pre-dawn hours a week or so later I found myself with Brent standing outside the door of the building that housed everyone's payroll records. We had parked the patrol truck and walked up to the door like we belonged, but I knew we should not be here.

For me, acting on revenge was akin to entering unfamiliar territory. It required a gigantic ethical leap. I wasn't brought up that way and Brent's proposal and my agreement ignited the raging fires of Catholic guilt, sometimes dormant, but ever present just beneath the surface.

Feelings working overtime, I had been engaged in a moral tennis match over the past week, batting sentiments back and forth.

First: "This is exactly what I should do to this woman-stealing jerk off and it serves him right."

Then: "I can't do this. It's dead wrong and it's really going to screw this guy up."

I was searching for a way to do the deed yet not feel guilty about it. Much as I tried, I never could quite let go of my nagging conscience.

So, here I was, stomach cartwheeling as I skulked around, looking about to see if anyone would spot us. We entered the building with flashlights, locked the door behind us and made our way to the payroll section. The records were inside an interior room, so it was safe to turn on the lights. The documents in metal filing cabinets were filed alphabetically, so it didn't take long to find our man's folder.

The plan was to grab his binder, remove it and destroy it. It would create a snafu that he would only belatedly discover on payday when he didn't receive his expected pay check. The administration would be unable to find his records and with military red tape being what it was, it would take some time to sort out. He'd get paid eventually, but not when he expected it. That would cause him some suffering.

My good angel began once again to whisper in my ear, so I said, "Hey Brent, you know what, I'm not feeling comfortable doing this. Let's forget it and get out of here."

"Are you kidding? C'mon, this guy deserves it, alright?"

"Yeah, maybe," I said, "but I just don't think it's right."

I said that even as the devil on my other shoulder sighed, "You know you want to do this."

In the end, he won out.

When Brent opened a drawer, I didn't try to stop him.

"Well, look what I found," he said, triumphantly holding a folder aloft. "C'mon let's get the lights and get out of here."

As wrong as it was and with as much self-reproach as I had ever felt, a part of me smiled inside. I had hit back at someone who I believed was the central cause for my deep anguish. It never occurred to me then that this guy was probably doing me a favor and maybe my great love didn't run so deeply after all.

All these years later I can remember this incident like it was yesterday—that's how deep the ethical battle was. And all these years later I know I lost that struggle. What I did took me to a dark place. Another one of my not-proudest moments that I still consider to be one of my lowest points, proving my Catholic guilt runs deep, indeed.

Sure the guy got paid eventually, no doubt. But in many ways my wrong-headed action was so much worse than his. For me to stoop that low and go out of the way to hurt another human in an act of retaliation went against everything I was made of. Hell, at that time I still was occasionally concerned about hurting people when I had to get physical during an arrest.

In the long run, acting upon that revenge didn't really ease the sorrow of losing a fiancée. In the end, not only had I lost her, I had lost some of my own self-respect, and that was just as taxing.

20

NO BULLETS, NO PEACE

DURING THOSE DAYS I was always surrounded by a variety of interesting people from all manner of backgrounds. Many of us gained new nicknames from our buddies overseas. For instance, there was Dave Worthen, from Illinois, who was large bodied, over 6-feet tall and had dark brown hair sweeping across his forehead.

Dave early on earned the moniker of "Trashcan" thanks to his prodigious appetite for beer. Many a time after work, we cops would grab a green 55-gallon trash can, load in a case or three of beer and fill it with ice. Dave, aka Trash, was the squadron's Hoover vacuum of beer drinking.

He'd grab a can in a massive fist, rip off the tab and guzzle that sucker down practically in one motion. Then he'd reach for another. He didn't even start slowing down until he had drunk nearly a six-pack. Ala, Trashcan.

Tom Collins, a skinny, crazy Kentuckian with light, curly brown hair was the one who named Trash. Tom was a ringleader for all the right and mostly wrong reasons. He was a flight chief, aka the shift boss, who did his job and whom we followed. Tom also enjoyed the party life big time and some of us followed him down that road too. You can see why I liked him.

Back in those days of our youth, we had great capacity to tie one on, as they say, recover quickly and pop right back up, ready for more excitement. That scenario occurred more often than not.

On one memorable occasion, Tom was still so drunk when he reported for work, the armory refused to issue him bullets for his handgun. Turned out, that was a wise decision.

The story began when we got off work the day before and by early evening had hopped aboard the CCK Smoker headed to town. After all these years, I no longer recall where we went or what we did—and likely didn't remember much of it the next day either. But we had a hell of a good time, likely bar hopping on the Dozen, that stretched over the entire night.

We grabbed taxis back to base in the early morning hours, showered up and dressed to report to work by 6:45 a.m. We always lined up in formation, known as guardmount, for a briefing and sometimes an inspection just before work started.

Before lining up we had to go to the armory to each draw a .38-caliber Smith & Wesson revolver. Tom, who also could put away mass quantities of alcohol, entered the building weaving and reeking of booze. He stumbled to the counter as we watched, wondering if he should even have a gun.

"Sgt. Collins, are you OK?" the armory sergeant asked with a raised eyebrow.

"Me, yeah, I'm fine. Gimme my gun," Tom managed to spit out.

"Uh huh," the counterman said.

He pulled out a handgun, checked to make sure it was unloaded and passed it across the counter to Tom as he worked to scribble his name between the lines on the sign-out form.

Tom took the gun. "Where's the bullets?" he asked.

"You know what Sgt. Collins, I'm going to hang onto those for a while. Maybe you can come back in a couple of hours and we'll see."

"Ah man, that's bullshit. Give me my bullets."

But the armory man remained unmoved. He refused to yield. It turned out he was prescient.

"Ah, shit," Tom said, turning away, pushing through a few of us and walking to the armory door.

"Look out, I'm armed and dangerous," he yelled.

He raised the gun in the air and made shooting sounds.

"Koo-chew, koo-chew," he bellowed, as he pulled on the trigger.

In an unexpected quick motion he chopped the gun down and smashed it into the window on the armory's door, cracking the thick glass.

We didn't know whether to laugh or put him in cuffs, but at least he didn't have bullets.

Nonetheless, as a group we decided to intervene to prevent injury to himself and especially to innocent bystanders. We convinced him to dodge guardmount and then stay inside at the desk sergeant's desk to keep everyone out of the line of fire.

He didn't like the resolution, but he acquiesced. Another good thing. Most of the morning his astonishing greeting to anyone who happened to walk through the door frightened a couple of folks.

"Hey," he'd shout, when they entered the room.

Tom then jumped out of his chair, unholstered his pistol and pointed it at the unsuspecting visitor and pulled the trigger a few times.

"Koo-chew, koo-chew, koo-chew."

We quickly decided he needed way more supervision before word of his outlandish actions climbed the chain of command, so we got him to go lay down.

This brand of craziness was the kind of idiocy that could only happen in the military during this time. As bad as the previous-night's party group felt for a good part of that day, guess what we did right after work? We hopped on the CCK Smoker and headed back to town for another round of carousing. This time, we were smart enough to get back to base to capture some shut eye before work the next day.

We tended to gravitate towards fun wherever and whenever we could in 1971 at CCK, but sometimes that amusement took a back seat to the tangible, deep-seated difficulties among us. For a few years now racial problems between White and Black Americans had been brewing pretty much everywhere, and it was escalating.

James Earl Ray had assassinated Martin Luther King Jr. on April 4, 1968. In the aftermath, riots erupted across the U.S. in what some historians have called the greatest wave of social unrest since the Civil War.

Some of the demonstrations were peaceful, but not all. At the time of King's assassination, I was in basic training and we weren't even told about the killing, perhaps to reduce the potential for problems exploding within our own ranks. It would be years before I would learn of the extent of the demonstrations in the aftermath of King's murder.

Up until now I had personally not experienced or seen major problems erupt between Black and White GIs. But in Vietnam, I got my first real taste of the approaching storm during one of our nightly beer fests. A soul brother I had tipped a few beers with got real frank and in my face when I told him I was toying with the notion of becoming a civilian cop back in the World.

"You know, man, I'm digging this police thing. I'm thinking about being a cop when I get out. I like the excitement and every day is different. You never know what's coming," I told my drinking companion.

"Oh yeah man, is that right? Let me tell you something, you might want to think some on that."

"Really, why's that?" I asked.

"Cause if you did me wrong out there, I'd pull a piece and waste your ass in a minute if I had to," he said, peering at me without even a hint of a smile.

I jerked my head back slightly with raised eyebrows. I squinted just a little and searched his face. He's kidding, right? Where's the punchline? Where's the grin?

"What? C'mon man, you're shittin' me. You'd kill me? You don't mean that. You don't even know me that well. You wouldn't do that, c'mon."

He tilted his head slightly to the right. "Knowing you don't mean nothing. You a honkey cop, you'd be in my sights.

It was, to me, a chilling but very real declaration. I knew he was not screwing around and meant what he said. Don't remember partying with him much after that.

Reflecting the dynamics of what was happening back in the states, racial tension had been rising for months around CCK and in Taichung when I returned. Isolated confrontations between Black and White airmen began to occur more frequently.

Some Chinese held their own prejudices against Blacks and eventually we heard more about problems and assaults between those two cultural groups, too. Response from the military brass seemed to be tepid at best.

Around this time it hit me that I had basically been clueless about the volatile brew bubbling just underneath the relationships myself and other White guys had with the Black dudes. That mix exploded in the early summer of 1971 during three days of violence and destruction on the air base.

Tensions continued to boil slowly until some incident or confrontation on base, now obscured by time, sparked an explosion. Small groups gathered and began acting out. People were beaten and rioters torched vehicles and trashed buildings, prompting the base honchos to board up many windows. At one point, someone lowered the American flag in front of the headquarters building and yanked a Black Power flag with clenched-fist emblem skyward.

All of the cops were scrambling to respond and from there on it was cat chasing mouse. The chaos grew so intense, the Chinese who were the landlords of the base took unprecedented steps. The Asian brass confronted the American brass with a no-nonsense promise to send in their own fully-armed troops to quell the turbulence if the Americans couldn't stop it. That encounter happened right about the time we cops went on a kind-of strike.

As the violence exploded and kept on going, we were put on 12-hour shifts. It was wild, with one crazy call to respond to trouble following another, hour after hour.

It seemed the radio never stopped chattering warnings of general mayhem: "Vehicle fire front of K-243 Barracks. Windows broken out in the admin building. Group of people fighting in

NO BULLETS, NO PEACE

the lobby of the bowling alley. Dumpster fire behind the mess hall. Shots fired near the hospital."

By the time we got off duty in the early morning after nearly 72 hours of this insanity, we were all exhausted and fed up. It felt like the powers-that-be had lost control and that we were on our own and no one had our backs. We couldn't see a solution ahead and at the time we were unaware of the intervention threats by the Chinese military.

At the end of that last overnight shift, we gathered in the day room of our barracks and collectively decided drastic action was needed or nothing was going to change anytime soon. So, we decided to go send a message and be real public about it, too. Whoever had the barracks room facing the street threw open windows and ran wires outside into two giant, 100-watt speakers. Inside he fired up a quadraphonic amplifier and a turntable. A few dozen of us gathered outside on the front lawn. A couple of the inevitable 55-gallon green trash cans materialized, which were promptly filled with beer and ice.

As Country Joe McDonald blared out his famous anti-war anthem "I-Feel-Like-I'm-Fixing-To-Die Rag," someone lit a couple of reefers and started passing them around. When it got to the chorus of "Give me an F, give me a U . . ." we all sang loudly and with fervor.

It was morning, probably around 9 a.m. and the sun was rising higher, promising the usual scorcher of a Taiwan day. I stood in a circle with a few other guys and inhaled deeply as the joint came my way. Other shirtless barrack mates in shorts dragged chairs out onto the lawn. The sound of popping beer pull tabs accompanied Country Joe.

Everyone was exhausted after running from flare up to flare up over the past days, sometimes literally putting out fires. Our little protest was triggering a big release valve, letting us blow off steam and anger. And we were taking a collective deep breath as we got blasted on beer, weed and rollicking rock-n'-roll.

We also understood that the audacity of protesting on-base police would send a graphic message to everyone from the shit disturbers all the way up to the sit-on-their-behinds brass—"go fuck yourselves all of you" was our outlook at the moment.

The hot sun and free-flowing party substances started working their magic. Tight wires of tension began to loosen up. I slumped back in a chair as the music washed over my weary body and mind. I thought of home, which after three years in Asia seemed like it was from another lifetime in another dimension.

The wayward festivities eventually attracted enough notice to warrant a visit from our police commander and an aide who pulled up in a jeep. I tensed up, unsure of what might be coming next. Whatever it was, it wasn't likely to be good. But if it was court martial and jail time, so be it. Who would take us in and to where? We were the police and the police were on strike.

"Wada they gonna do, send me to Vietnam? Been there, done that," was kind of my thought process.

Our commander, recognizing the potential volatility of the situation I think, was wise enough to avoid the typical military bulldozer approach of plowing through a problem to eliminate said problem. He made no demands or threats.

He understood the stress and strain of three days of acute upheaval on us. He talked things over with a couple of our ranking guys. And that was it. He assured us measures were underway to get the base calmed down.

Thank you Chinese landlords! Meanwhile, he told us to have fun, keep the craziness under control and get some rest. Time in the brig was not in the mix today, nor another trip to Vietnam. He got it.

And though our little strike had no real effect, as far as I know, tempers cooled and the violence stopped without the Chinese activating their troops.

21
DOPES ON DOPE

RACIAL TROUBLES and turmoil weren't the only rising difficulties at CCK around this time. Illegal drugs, especially marijuana, had become very much a part of life for many, a radical shift from our previous lives back home where drugs played little, if any, role. It was new and fun and exciting!

Part of the thrill was the escape of military drudgery and part of it was simply enjoyment, laughing with friends and listening to great music while developing a close camaraderie with the buddies who passed a lit joint your way.

Taiwan's martial law government didn't screw around when it came to illegal drug use, so the island itself was not a resource for dope. But that steely toughness didn't stop weed from showing up on base. The drug pipeline for CCK, especially for marijuana, ran through the airways traversed by our aircraft.

Drugs in other Southeast Asian ports were easily accessed by some visiting flying crews who loaded up their planes for the return trip. It could be risky but those willing to take the chance knew inspections were not heavy handed at the time. Some of those inspectors were cops who also liked to get high, so mutually beneficial relationships were developed.

The whole air mail delivery scenario was the worst kept "secret" on the base. It seemed like everyone knew it, including the military chiefs eventually. That knowledge certainly had to rub the brass the wrong way. This was illegal behavior and it had to stop, so they acted.

The military launched what I'll call Operation Crackdown, although I don't know if it had a real name. They brought in dogs trained to sniff out pot; they turned up the heat on incoming aircraft, requiring thorough examinations of every bird that landed.

These new enforcement activities alarmed the party class, aka "the heads." The measures might choke off the flow of marijuana, but it would also open the door to importation of a far more dangerous and addictive drug—heroin. Heroin, an opioid also known as smack, snow, horse, junk and skag, was more compact, far easier to hide and much more difficult, if not impossible, for dope-sniffing-trained dogs to detect at the time.

Some farsighted airmen understood that bored young males stuck so far from home and accustomed to easy access to party materials were going to find illicit relief one way or another if that flow of weed stopped. With limited or no access to pot, the temptation to try heroin would be irresistible for some.

One day a couple of guys in the hospital squadron publicly advertised that concern by painting a large sign that they then planted on the front lawn of their barracks that said, "Let's fuck the war + smack. We need herb."

That radical display ticked off the brass and the next day an Inspector General paid a personal visit to the guys in that squadron to try to sniff out the culprits. The gumshoes got squat.

A few other sages took the rare step of approaching the base honchos. Their mission was to sound the alarm and try to make the bosses see that closing off the marijuana pipeline would only generate a flood of "white death" in the form of heroin. I wasn't part of the negotiating team, but it was well known throughout the base grapevine that these concerns were carried to CCK's top dogs.

But of course the military was not going to say, "No problem, just bring in as much illegal dope as you'd like, we'll look the other way." The chiefs executed their plans and that stream of weed quickly dried up, although not entirely. You can never underestimate the resourcefulness and creativity of those desperate to get high as a Georgia pine.

When the clampdown got underway one fella close to C-130 crew members told me, "All you gotta do is say 'I got a bunch of dope I need to get to CCK.' You'll get a guy on every screw on the top of a wing, they'll take it off, fill it up with weed and screw it back together."

That's not a scenario I witnessed, and as crazy and dangerous as it sounds, I have no way of knowing if it actually occurred. That said, considering the times, it's not totally outside the realm of possibility. The stuff was still coming in, just less frequently, creating a bigger demand and a robust seller's market.

What I do know is the guys who pleaded for the brass to rethink things were correct. Suddenly, skag was everywhere. And it became wildly popular. Its euphoric high gave users an initial "rush" of pleasurable sensations, enhanced greatly when the person injected it into their veins.

The drug's effects would flush a user's skin, dry up their mouth and launch heavy waves of drowsiness across their body for hours. A strong enough dose and it was nighty-night time.

No wonder heroin is so highly addictive. Once a regular

user grows accustomed to doses, their body will revolt when it doesn't get a fix. I watched guys get restless, jerky and shaky when they needed another hit. They'd sweat and then get cold flashes and pain in their muscles and bones. That intense body craving for the drug was known as "Jonesin'." Heroin use and addiction spread across the base. You'd think security policemen would just say no, but too many did not. Every day down the hall from my barracks room, a handful of cops gathered to hit it up. I'm not sure how those meetings started nor how they progressed, but for a while they were pretty regular. I was not one who attended the gathering.

It was easy enough to spot guys spiraling downward from the fallout of heroin use. The drug has a variety of ill effects, including acting as an appetite suppressant. Some users shrunk down to skin and bones, losing up to 40 or more pounds as they continued shooting up the drug.

And when a regular fix was interrupted, suffering would inevitably follow them no matter where they were. I remember one guy Jonesin' as he worked at the Main Gate where everyone, including the officers, entered and left the base. He didn't get caught because those of us who saw what was happening covered for him and got him off of the post before all hell broke loose.

The question I confront many years later is why? Why did we look the other way as some of our partners dropped headlong into heroin's hellish torment? Any one of us could have reported what was going on, but we didn't. I remember thinking these guys were crazy as they gathered for their down-the-hall buzz.

But they were also part of the police brotherhood, with its code of good cops remaining blind and silent to their colleagues' bad-cop behavior. It's a well-known phenomenon, alive then as it is today.

Maybe a part of that was also an us-against-them mentality. Maybe some of it was sheer stupidity, but none of the cops who knew what was going on turned in any of their associates for drug abuse as far as I know.

We closed ranks, I think, because we worked together closely, but also because most of the users were decent guys, albeit with an illegal and dangerously awful habit. Looking back, it was wrong and a sad situation in so many ways. People deteriorated before our eyes, but no one turned into a snitch while I was on base, or at least I was unaware if anyone did.

It was also a different and difficult time. While I didn't condone the daily heroin use, I had done my own share of partying. I drank, smoked pot, had tried hashish and had even sipped opium-laced hot chocolate. And in truth, I was also curious about the buzz hooking so many around me. So I tried it too.

I knew this drug could quickly turn into a beast of an addiction so I was cautious and tentative when I stepped into treacherous territory to give it a try. No way would I ever grab a needle and inject this rocket fuel into my veins.

Someone offered me a cigarette laced with smack and I gave it a few puffs. I immediately understood why heroin was so popular. I went right to la-la land without passing go. Later on I also snorted a line or two to see what that would do. It did pretty well, alright. But I knew I had to draw the line at no more lines after these experiments or I would be sharing a seat in the junkie boat with some of the miserable, wasting away hooked guys that surrounded me.

Sadly, a few of them took the ultimate trip when they shot up junk. More than a couple of wide-eyed users who messed around with smack back in the World were thrilled with the ease of obtaining the drug when they landed at CCK. Unfortunately, they badly misjudged the potency of this vicious White Horse, which was considerably stronger than what they were used to. Back home, dealers stepped on heroin with baking soda, starch, powdered milk or even talcum or baby powder. At CCK, the stuff was 85 percent pure or higher. A few guys discovered the difference the hard way and overdosed.

A couple of them died.

22

BACK TO THE DOZEN

EAGER TO GET OUT of the bedlam and craziness of the base, I lobbied hard to get back on Town Patrol, pitching the value of my previous experience from back in 1969. Eventually, my bosses either saw the light or they simply got tired of my pleas, although being that it was the military, the latter was unlikely.

At any rate, I was reassigned back to Town Patrol in spring 1972. By that time, the military had jettisoned the Hostel as living quarters. We were provided an increased per diem to rent an apartment in town, which was great and easily affordable in the local economy. Ten dollars in Taiwanese money was basically 25 cents, U.S.

Our outfit had also lost our Chinese drivers by this time and we had switched from the Navy Econovans to Air Force paddy wagons. The job itself had changed little, if at all. We parked the truck in the same old spot on Wu Chan Lu in the heart of the Dirty Dozen outside of one of our favorite eateries, the P.C.S. Snack Bar. After we walked through the bars to ensure all was well, we would sit in the van, waiting for trouble to raise its angry head. We rarely waited long.

Traffic around town and on the island was still horrendous and we continued to devote a lot of working time to covering accidents—from fender benders to some horrific fatal crashes.

It seemed more Americans than ever drove and lived off base, so we also answered our share of domestic disputes and breaking and entering—B&E—calls. A thriving black market also grabbed our attention. The military tried to control the purchases of things like cigarettes, beer, liquor and even large appliances, such as stoves and refrigerators. U.S. dollars were also a big deal—allegedly it was illegal to buy any local products and pay with American money, but that was a hard one to enforce.

The booze and smokes were the hottest items on the black market. On more than a couple of occasions, "Let's-take-his-pay-records" Brent, who now had also moved to TAFP, and I went undercover in our civilian clothes to haunt the liquor store and BX, looking to catch a GI selling these restricted items to a Chinese buyer. We nabbed a few for illegal sales of liquor and cigarettes to the locals. It felt kind of cool to skulk around in our civvies, on alert for potential law breakers.

Another thing that had not changed since 1969 was the popularity of the Dirty Dozen. The bars served their purpose for allowing American servicemen to blow off steam, maybe find a girlfriend and wake up the next day with a pounding hangover. The mix of guys was still the same: most were from the base, intermingled with the grunts on R&R from Vietnam who had either come in on our C-130s or had flown first to Taipei and then come south to Taichung, beckoned by less competition for dates and cheaper prices all around compared to the capital.

Trouble was ever present and we never knew what form it would take when it came rolling up to us in a night. As I said before, it was often the little guys who presented challenges. Many always seemed ready to duke it out rather than comply peacefully.

The bigger fellows often, not always of course, seemed more willing to cooperate. There was one unforgettable exception, however.

My partner Ray Hernandez and I were sitting in the van during a quiet moment when a taxi suddenly squealed around the front of our vehicle and came to a sudden stop, kicking up rocks and dirt.

The Chinese driver jumped out and started yakking excitedly and pointing toward his back seat. We got out, walked over to the taxi and saw a rather large human with his head leaning against the back window on the passenger side, obviously passed out.

We carefully opened the door and started shaking his right shoulder.

"Hey man, wake up. Are you OK?" Ray asked.

We kept saying "hey man" loudly and shaking him but he was out of it. Ray pulled out a capsule of amyl nitrate, encased in glass that was covered in cloth. Medically they are used to relieve pain of angina attacks.

Also known as "poppers," some people used them for an instant, laugh-filled high or to improve sex. For us, they were one of the few tools we carried and we used them to deliver a jolt to the brain of passed-out drunks. You would break the capsule in half and hold it under a blacked-out guy's nose and let it work its magic. And boy, did it work! In this case, the passenger jerked his head up immediately, and with arms flailing, he rose out of that drunken coma like someone lit a torch under his ass.

"C'mon man, you got to get out of there. Where are you going? Let's see your ID."

He mumbled something unintelligible back at us but made no move to get out of the back seat. We reached down and muscled him out of the taxi and into a standing position, but just barely. He was weaving and stumbling as we held onto his arms. He was a big guy and carried some bulk on his body.

Because he was shit-faced drunk, Ray and I knew this one was a keeper. We finessed him awkwardly toward the back of our paddy wagon and got one door open. Seeing the wired cage at the back of our truck must have been another wake-up call. Suddenly he was animated with kinetic energy before we could even open the other door.

He whirled and swung his arms as we held on and struggled to maintain control. We hadn't handcuffed him because up to now he had been docile. Ray was a pretty solid guy himself and I could hold my own, but this was like hanging onto some kind of weird, powerful, whip-like octopus ride.

We finally managed to get him face up against the closed door and get his arms behind his back to cuff him. Most guys would quit at that point, but not this buffoon. He had only just begun.

Several times we wrestled him into the open doorway of the vehicle, but he fought furiously and we could never get him and all of his body parts fully into the back of the cage. Every time we got close to getting him all the way in, he managed to get a knee or a foot in the door jamb, preventing us from closing the door. One time he got his fingers in the doorway!

"Arrrrrgggghhhhh," he yelled.

"Ray, watch it, his damn fingers are in the door," I yelled.

By this point we had tried everything, including me punching him in the balls. But this drunk just kept on thrashing, kicking both Ray and me numerous times. He was so loaded, he wasn't feeling a thing.

If you've never been in a prolonged struggle or fight, I can tell you it sucks the energy right out of you. It doesn't take very long before you are exhausted. We battled on trying to subdue him for what seemed like an hour, but in reality was likely closer to under five minutes. Both Ray and I were whipped.

With hands on our knees, we paused to catch our breaths. The resister was sprawled with his upper body half on the floor of the cage and his legs dangling outside over the rear bumper. I looked at him and the solution hit in an instant.

Per usual, it wasn't necessarily the smartest idea, but we couldn't keep going like this. Had to stop the madness, so I acted.

I rushed him, scooped up both of his legs and kept moving forward until both he and I were in the truck's cage in the back, me half on the floor and half on the bench with my arms wrapped around his legs in a weird embrace.

"Shut the door, shut the door," I screamed to Ray.

"TC, you sure? This is crazy, let him go and get out," Ray said.

The guy wasn't struggling much if at all at this point, but I was afraid if I let him go he'd follow me right back out before we could close the door and we'd be back to square one.

"No, it's OK, I got him, shut the door and let's go."

He was cuffed, I somehow managed to turn him around so he was half laying and sitting on the bench, arms behind his back so what's the worry, I thought. I felt confident I could handle him in this position, but I failed to consider one perilous prospect.

We were driving back to the Navy Compound, Ray constantly turning to check on me, when somewhere along the route my inebriated seatmate projectile vomited right at me and down the front of my khakis.

Oh man, I had to ride the rest of the way to HQ with his barf dripping down my chest. I was barely able to keep myself from puking the rest of the ride back to our building.

When Ray parked in front of our office and opened the door, I shot out of there like a rocket, deeply inhaling fresh air. We yanked the dude out of the vehicle, expecting more trouble. But by now his condition had the best of him so we got him in our tiny holding cell without further incident.

The next day I had a few giant bruises on my arms and chest from getting kicked. Luckily, he had not connected with our heads.

Lesson? Not every big guy, especially a drunk one, was as docile as Bambi. Oh, and don't get in a moving vehicle in a tight space with a totally smashed person.

23
SOARING SENTINELS AND BAR BEEFS

TYPHOON RITA BEGAN to form southeast of Guam in July 1972, which proved to be a remarkably active month for tropical storms. It would be just one of four cyclones dancing around the Pacific that month, but Rita was the queen of the ball.

She blew long and heavy, wreaking havoc for 22 days with winds howling as high as 167 miles per hour at one point. Rita was indeed a Super Typhoon and would become one of the longest-lived storms in the western Pacific.

All of these gales swirling around in the ocean presented a potential for major trouble should they slam into Taiwan. It was a crapshoot, but the military, not willing to gamble with equipment worth multi millions of dollars, initiated its standard batten-down-the hatches routine. Pilots jumped aboard their aircraft and evacuated the island for safer territory.

Meanwhile, each squadron on the base worked hard to latch down anything appearing to be insecure. As Rita drew nearer and as we always did in similar situations, we began our sweep of the Dirty Dozen and the bars outside of it to send airmen packing for home in preparation for the potential devastation headed our way.

As it turned out, Rita blew by us without a direct hit, but the storm was so powerful its proximity pummeled the island with violent gusts of wind and dumped 15 inches of rain in some areas.

MADE IN TAIWAN

During normal times our office would shut down for a few hours beginning very early in the morning after the bars had closed and our patrols were over for the night. Typhoons changed that norm—seven of them rammed the island while I was there—and we began pulling 12-hour shifts.

As the evening progressed, the worsening storm wiped out all electrical power. We had cleared the town and shut down the bars, so we were hunkered down in our small office inside the Navy Compound.

A couple of times my partner Joe Blaise ventured out into the crazy weather to check on the buildings in the Compound, including the commissary, the military version of a civilian grocery store.

During one check around midnight, we discovered the store's back-up generator had failed and wind had torn a small hole in the roof of the building. Water was leaking inside. We couldn't call the store manager because Rita had wiped out phone service, too.

The only option was to jump in the truck and drive to his house to alert him, a risky-but-necessary venture for sure. Joe and I and a Chinese local cop saddled up and drove out of the compound to go alert the manager.

With Joe driving, we survived the trip without incident. When we pulled up to the manager's house I nervously jumped out of the vehicle—my foolhardy streak still alive and well, for now at least—to go pound on this guy's front door. Perhaps it's obvious, but it is really hard to remain upright in a typhoon-strength gale, let alone walk in a straight line.

Meanwhile, tree limbs, trashcans, lids, garbage and any and all debris that was even a little loose whipped by and around me.

SOARING SENTINELS AND BAR BEEFS

I became seriously frightened as I did my best to watch out for flying objects and duck if need be.

I staggered through the winds and rain, hands and arms cradled around my head just waiting for some unpleasant and dangerous item to bowl me over.

I reached the porch unscathed, banged on the door and roused the manager. I told him about the commissary's problems and he thanked me and told me to be careful, which was great advice, of course, but not super helpful considering the situation. I managed to make it back to the truck without getting mowed down by flying rubble.

Our vehicle rocked side to side and was battered with a pounding rain as we made our way slowly back toward our office, dodging the typhoon-generated flak along the way.

As we approached the Navy Compound entrance on our left, Joe slammed on the brakes. I grabbed the dashboard to avoid having my head bang into the windshield and simultaneously dropped my jaw at what I was witnessing.

Just inside the entrance gate, Chinese sentries would normally hang out in a mid-sized Quonset hut to take a break or to use as a shelter. With the ferocity of this storm, they obviously had headed inside for protection from the elements. But as we neared that gate, a vicious gust of wind somehow lifted that guard shack straight up off the ground.

There it was, airborne, right in front of us. It barely cleared the stone wall as it was blown above and across the road. Think of the twister that picked up Dorothy's house in the *Wizard of Oz*. The shack crashed down into slats of wooden fencing on the right side of the street. Wow! What came next was even more shocking.

MADE IN TAIWAN

Within moments of the crash, three Chinese men, some wearing only white T-shirts and shorts, staggered out of the smashed shack one by one. A couple of them had managed to don helmets, which sat askew on their heads.

All of them looked like they were drunk or had just stepped off a whirling, out-of-control amusement park ride. At the moment, they clearly didn't know where they were or what had hit them.

After the momentary shock lapsed, we quickly rolled down the windows to check on them. Our Chinese partner Sgt. Chen shouted questions in their direction. Besides some bumps and minor cuts, he told us the men seemed OK and were more bewildered than banged up. What a ride that must have been!

Those guys now had the story of their lifetimes. They were lucky and it was a funny tale that got funnier the more we told it. While no one was seriously injured in that incident, Rita did leave her mark on the island.

The storm derailed a train in southern Taiwan, triggered landslides, flooded villages and left 700 people homeless. During its reign of terror across the Pacific, the typhoon killed 229 people and became the deadliest storm of the season.

Mother Nature could create considerable disruption, but it wasn't the only fear-inducing turmoil we faced during my second year working downtown on Taichung Armed Forces Police in 1972. Racial rancor continued to raise its ugly head and it wasn't always a White and Black thing. As I mentioned earlier, some Chinese were prejudiced against Black Americans and some of the bars segregated themselves.

Those saloons preferred to cater to mostly White servicemen. Occasionally one of the bar owners would express that discriminatory attitude by telling their employees to slow walk the service or even ignore a Black customer as much as possible.

Many soul brothers often hung out in Bar Town, the area with fewer taverns which was about a 10-minute drive from the Main Gate on the CCK Smoker. It was smaller than Wu Chan Lu's Dirty Dozen and while we did patrol the area, it was quieter and any difficulties requiring our response were rarer. But racial issues did arise on The Dozen from time to time.

One night a Chinese girl ran up to our truck obviously agitated, yammering at our local police colleagues who relayed that a large group of Black Americans were crowded inside the Hollywood Club.

They weren't creating any kind of disturbance but they also weren't ordering anything. It was one of those infrequent occasions where I didn't have an American partner, so a Chinese MP, a local policeman and I hot-footed it to the bar.

Sure enough, 15-20 Black guys were crammed inside, occupying the bar and the tables. Except for soul music streaming from the jukebox, it was weirdly quiet. As we entered the bar, mama-san began jabbering loudly to my Chinese partners, filling them in on what was happening as I took stock of everyone around the place and they eyeballed me back.

"Sgt. Brown, these men all come here, just sit. They take up space in bar and don't buy anything. No room for someone else to come in now; no one buy anything. This not good for bar business," Sgt. Muyang Wu of the Chinese local police told me.

"Alright, got it," I said, turning to look at a few of the fellows nearest me at the bar, quietly watching. "OK guys, what's going on? You can't just come in here and take over the place and not spend money. What are you doing?"

My words opened the floodgates. Everybody started talking or yelling at once. These guys were pissed off but I wasn't yet sure about what.

"Hey, hey, calm down. What the hell is the problem?" I asked.

I began to sweat the situation. The place was packed with angry Black airmen and I was a lone White cop with a couple of Chinese partners. If their wrath really boiled over, this was not going to end well for the guys with the badges.

Then one guy stepped forward, becoming the de facto spokesman for the group. He got the others to tone it down and he told me their side of the story as he and I stood in front of the jukebox.

He said that the night before a couple of brothers had come to the Hollywood Club and were unable to get service. They were angry and went back to the base and told their friends what had happened. Word spread and that story was enough to motivate a large group to return tonight for a sit-in. If they couldn't get served, no one else was going to get served either.

I told the narrator I understood why they were pissed off but I also tried to reason, pointing out that taking over a bar, even peacefully, wouldn't resolve or change what had happened the night before. I hoped to try to find some way to solve this without the whole situation blowing up and people getting hurt, especially me.

My logic seemed reasonable to me but truth be told, I wasn't confident I could say or do anything that would calm the waters. In reality, all I managed to do was poke an already pissed-off bear when I said, "Look, you can't just sit here and not buy anything." These men were mad as hell and didn't want to hear that comeback.

Several guys shouted at once: "Yeah, what you gonna do about it, huh? You gonna arrest us all? You all going to kick us out, make us buy something? Go ahead and try."

Frustration escalated and people were starting to get worked up even more. I could sense this combustible setting was on the verge of spinning way out of control, but I was at a loss.

I knew I couldn't try to arrest anyone. They would pulverize me and run. There was no way I could make them leave, either. It was Mexican standoff time.

The looming hostility pushed me into previously unexplored territory and at a loss for what to do, I unwittingly launched a tactic I'll call "out-crazy-the crowd." I was mad, too, and sick of all the racial animosity over the past couple of years.

I felt kinship with many of these guys I had met these past four years and one of them—Al Hoover—had even anointed me with the nickname I had happily and fully adopted by now.

I looked at the guy standing next to me who had explained why everyone was camped out in the bar in the first place.

"Know what, the hell with it. Tear the place apart if you want, I don't give a shit," I said, whipping off my white police cap and slamming it down on the jukebox. "I can't stop you guys from doing what you want, so have fun. I'm tired of this bullshit. But tell you what, this is only going to get bad for you later if you tear this place up."

I was not trying to be a tough-guy hero here. I just didn't know how else to play it without creating more serious problems, leading to violence. And frankly, I was scared at what might break out here. So I let my gut lead the way on this one.

I have no recollection how my Chinese partners reacted to this irrational response from me, but I sure as hell surprised the Americans. They looked at me, some in wide-eyed amazement, if not shock. Clearly my outlandish comeback had not been anticipated. I was pretty surprised my own self at what had come out of my mouth.

"Hey, hey, brothers wait a minute. Wait. Let's hear my man out here. Listen up," the spokesman said.

And oddly enough, they did. Time has eroded the conversation that he and I had after that, but somehow this guy's calming words and my half-witted, gut-lead response worked their magic, and a once-volatile situation was defused peacefully.

Some guys began filtering out while a few hung around. Miraculously, I managed to escape this sticky mess without getting my ass kicked or seeing a local tavern thoroughly trashed. It was a great lesson: pay heed to your instincts.

It wasn't always Americans causing problems on The Dozen. The Chinese had their own share of scalawags, and if they chose to create difficulty and disturbances where Americans played, we were called for help.

One unforgettable occasion began, as they often did, when a frantic Chinese man ran up to us on the strip, waving his arms and yelling to our local partners.

"Big fight at Wagon Wheel," our Chinese MP Sgt. Yichen Shih announced.

With that alert, we were off, four of us running down the street to the bar as fast as we could. When we ran like this it was awkward—I had to hang onto my black baton in its ring holster to keep it from beating bruises on my right calf.

The Wagon Wheel bar was on the second story, so we hustled up a long flight of stairs and by the time we got to the top I was winded.

After all this time on Town Patrol, I thought I couldn't be surprised by any incident, but I had never seen this one: two Chinese men were wildly swinging long bamboo poles, demolishing the bottles and glasses that were on and behind the bar.

They also took swipes at any person who was in range, so the few customers and employees were scrambling to give a wide berth as breaking glassware mingled with screams of fear.

Our Chinese partners bellowed some kind of drop-your-weapons order and it was enough to get the Bamboo Boys' attention. They stopped swinging the poles, but they didn't drop them.

We Americans weren't armed beyond our batons, and while the Chinese MPs carried sidearms, Sgt. Shih couldn't pull his weapon and start shooting without hitting innocent bystanders. Our own batons were way shorter than the whip-long weapons wielded by the Bamboo Boys. My heart was hammering as we started to move toward them.

Those poles looked like they could inflict serious harm because, of course, they could. Bamboo is the Superman of natural materials, with a tensile strength stronger than steel. The wood is three times stronger than timber.

The two attackers kept tables and chairs between us and them as the Chinese police stayed by the top of the steps to block their exit. The Boys shuffled their way through tables to the railing surrounding the top of the stairs. Our Chinese partners were yelling commands at them, but without hesitation first one and then the other straddled the bronze rail.

Hanging onto their poles, each dropped over the side to the middle of the steps. Surprisingly neither one of them broke a leg when they landed. Both bounded down the steps and out the front door, with us in hot pursuit.

They made it around a corner, jumped in a vehicle and were gone in a flash. If they were ever caught, it would have been by the local authorities later on. They had exacted serious damage on much of the barware, but everyone inside managed to avoid getting struck or injured.

Our partners told us the Boys launched the attack over a money dispute and that it involved a local gang. I was just happy no one got whipped upside their heads by a potentially lethal bamboo stick, including me.

24

PARTNERS, CLOWNS AND BETEL JUICE

I LIVED IN TAIWAN for nearly four years, separated not quite in the middle by my time in Vietnam. I can also divide that time by my two loves. Penny, the first young woman, moved on to someone else ripping out my heart in the process, and changed her American name to Anna.

Edie, my second love, was the young beauty that I let get away, unsure if I could or would be able to take her back home for a lasting marriage. That decision on my part likely caused Edie at least some of the same emotional damage inflicted on me by my former fiancée years before. What a flip flop by me. Love can be hard, yes?

My memory of when and where I met Edie is clouded with the fog of time. Her Chinese name was Mei Chen and she was part aborigine. I do know she also worked in one of the bars I frequented. I had met her before I returned to Town Patrol in the spring of 1972. Soon after I began to work in Taichung, we got an apartment together.

With the extra bonus of per diem money for working and living downtown, I was able to afford a decent sized, one-bedroom, third-floor apartment, which became a popular gathering spot for my buddies who still lived on base. At some point Edie quit working at the bar at my insistence and we became a household.

Edie was gorgeous, inside and out. She spoke and understood English well. She had a happy-go-lucky, bright and bubbly personality and absolutely adored children. That woman loved to laugh and clown around. Go to the beach, Edie would be the first to help you dig a hole so you could bury her up to her neck.

She constantly flashed a prominent wide toothy smile in her soft round face. She was native Taiwanese and her dark hair, which reached the middle of her back, was naturally streaked with light shades of brown and red throughout. She favored bright-colored clothing and often wore long, colorful beaded necklaces.

I know she was in love with me and I loved her back, for sure. What I didn't recognize at the time was that I hadn't fully recovered from my traumatic broken engagement with Penny.

And that dark shadow of doubt lurking within made me hesitant to commit fully to Edie, as it would do years in the future in other relationships. I couldn't help but harbor suspicion that maybe Edie, too, might not be faithful in the long run.

In the recesses of my mind, I feared she might pull the rug out from under this relationship at some point. As much as I cared about her, I didn't appreciate or recognize this sharp edge that cut through the bonds of our relationship at the time.

But for the most part, we were a happy couple and we traveled as much as we could. After I returned from Vietnam, I had purchased a blue Datsun that before long was nicknamed the "Dustmobile" by one of my smart-aleck friends due to its normal less-than-pristine condition.

Taiwan is filled with natural beauty and we loved to take trips to explore. Jagged mountains tower over 70 percent of the island, a mixture of lush jungle, hot springs and lava rock coastlines.

It offers scenic attractions like Sun Moon Lake or Taroko Gorge, but one of the most popular spots is Alishan National Scenic Area in Central Taiwan, where people flock to catch a magnificent mountain sunrise above a sea of clouds.

On one trip the Dustmobile took Edie and me to Chiayi near Alishan for an overnight stay. We arose before 4:00 a.m. the next morning so we could board a small forest train that chugged precariously—it seemed to us—up Mount Alishan through the cold, mist-shrouded forests.

Some of these woods are 2,000 years old. The view resembled many of the mystical scenes I'd seen in Chinese paintings. Unfortunately the train didn't go all the way to the summit, which tops out at nearly 9,000 feet. Once we got off, we had a killer hike that seemed to go straight up to the top of the mountain. And this was all before sunrise!

It was an icy, grueling trek and I wasn't quite sure I'd beat the sun to the top. But the sky was starting to lighten, which provided a reserve energy burst that somehow got me to the summit just before the sunrise.

As wiped out as I felt, it was a sight I'll never forget. When we stopped we were looking down on a lake of fluffy clouds nestled within mountain ranges. On the distant horizon, the sky began to light up with a pale pink haze that slowly turned red and then buttery as the top edge of the yellow ball of the sun rose over a swirling spray of clouds and the caps of the mountain ridges. It was the second time after that uphill trek that my breath was taken away.

During my years in Asia I met all assortment and manner of people, both American and Chinese, and many became close friends who hung out with Edie and me. During my last year in

Taiwan I became especially tight with three other Americans and we quickly became a group, much like I had done with the kids from the band in my high school days.

We were all sky cops until Rick Campbell transferred to the hospital squadron. We had become good friends when I was still on the base and that relationship didn't falter once I moved to Town Patrol.

Rick, Hal Thoms, Dave Kinney and myself became a fun-loving, goofy unit who called each other "Clown Kid." Rick had a square chin, a shock of curly red hair and a thick red mustache.

As I've mentioned, military nicknames were common (think Trash Can) so it didn't take long before Rick became "Red." Red hailed from the Bay Area. He had lettered in three sports in high school and had a physique that suggested he had once been a bad ass defensive end.

Hal came from Southern California and was the coolest guy any of us had ever met. He literally was a surfer dude in every sense of the word. He stood about 6-feet, 5-inches, wore large glasses and had a shock of light brown hair often cordoned off in the front with a blue visor emblazoned with an American flag emblem. He had an easy Southern California inflection and an almost child-like, laid-back way of looking at life, like everything was new or amazing or both. Hal's go-to reaction to most conditions was simple and slow: "Wow, man."

As a cop, Hal had found at least one way to put into practice the us-against-the-military mentality many of us embraced. When he stopped someone on base for running a stop sign or speeding, he would simply issue a warning if the offender was an enlisted man. For all officers, he issued traffic tickets.

PARTNERS, CLOWNS AND BETEL JUICE

Hal was a serial writer of letters to Marilyn, a woman he had never met but knew about through his sister. He was smitten to the core. He took up pursuit from a distance employing a thoughtful painstaking touch—he wrote each missive, often daily, in a different color of ink. It was both a unique and very cool quest. No wonder she married him when he went back home. Five decades later, they're still together.

Dave was an intense guy from Detroit with floppy brown hair, a long nose and a square chin. He looked as if he'd stepped out of a bodybuilding magazine way before such activity became a national craze. Dave had muscles on his muscles, with biceps large and powerful enough to crack walnuts.

Rounding out this group of misfits was Yichen Shih, a Chinese friend who had mastered English and was the coolest Chinese MP we had ever worked with on Town Patrol. He and I were often partnered on the job.

When on duty, Yichen was no-nonsense, spit-shined and sharp as a scalpel. He had to be to be selected as one of 10 Chinese MPs in a graduating class of about 100 to work in Taichung's Armed Forces Police detachment.

On the inside, Yichen was chill. He was a sponge, soaking up American culture. He fit in well and we "officially" made him a "Clown."

"Cloowwnnnn Kid!" became an identifier for each one of us oddballs, either as a term of endearment or an expression of shock when one of us said or did something spectacularly stupid or crazy, which occurred more often than not. I don't remember who invented that drawn-out epithet, but I suspect Hal was the instigator since he was often the de-facto leader of our escapades.

MADE IN TAIWAN

The expression likely grew out of a reaction to one of us being exceptionally silly: "What a clown." Don't ask me why now because I have no clue, but another expression of amazement or flattery was, "Kid, cad, code!"

It didn't make much sense, or really any sense for that matter, but it had a nice cadence. Somewhere along the way we combined the two phrases and created the signature Clown Kid. The rest is history. On the rare occasions when we talk even today, that silly greeting usually opens the conversation.

As different as our backgrounds, we all shared common interests. Much of our focus revolved around hanging out and listening to the music of the day, while getting high in a room filled with incense, lava lamps, Day-Glo posters and black lights.

For sure we were rebelling against the authority of the military and all of its rules and demands on our lives. So we were gonna do what made us feel good, legal or not.

But we were also escaping to a different world in our out-of-body-like experiences, real or not. The music (and weed) helped carry us to a place where people joined hands and worked together instead of fighting and hating one another. Where the love of living and life erased the dark angst or pain of the war and all it entailed that constantly intruded into our realities.

Yes, it was an escape. But we hopped aboard that head-trip tour on a regular basis. We enjoyed the hell out of those times and it tightened our bonds.

Stereo equipment, especially in those days, was dirt cheap because Japan was cranking out mountains of electronics like it still does. And the Land of the Rising Sun is relatively close to Taiwan, so we had many options.

PARTNERS, CLOWNS AND BETEL JUICE

I bought a Pioneer quadraphonic four-channel amplifier, a Teac reel-to-reel tape player, four Pioneer 80-watt speakers and a Sansui turntable. The equipment lasted for decades and still worked when I foolishly sold it many years later.

Anyway, as noted previously we spent a lot of time listening to record albums and tape recordings, which is how everyone got tunes in those days. Music was a central part of our lives, a bridge to the World, and we shared with each other our favorites from the buffet of albums we all owned.

But for us Clowns, the musical group that held the title for best band ever was the Moody Blues. Each of their albums highlighted a theme and provided its own head-trip journey.

After the Moody's rhythm and blues debut record, the English group began to fuse classical music with rock for its second "concept" album in 1967 called *Days of Future Past*.

No other band was creating this sort of progressive rock at the time. And we dug it, big time. So, every once in a while we picked a day and declared it to be International Moody Blues Day.

Of course, we had to plan and prepare for that big event. Translation: ensure we had enough party materials and munchies to last for hours. We could not interrupt festivities because we ran out of the goodies.

This momentous day would start in the morning with the Moody's second album. By this time, the group had released another six records and we listened to each album in chronological order. It could not be done in any other fashion.

There were so many songs, we had to take a break in the middle of the day before finally finishing up late with *Seventh Sojourn*, which was released in 1972. Flash forward many decades and I was given a rare opportunity to tell this story to Justin Hayward, the Moody's front man and lead singer.

The band was coming to Columbus, Ohio for a concert and I was assigned to conduct a pre-concert telephone interview for *The Columbus Dispatch*, where I worked as a feature writer. Justin and I talked about the band's development over the years and the upcoming show.

But just before we hung up, I told him the story of International Moody Blues Day long ago in a small city in the middle of Taiwan. Justin cracked up and told me it was one of the coolest band stories he'd ever heard. I like to think he shared that with bandmates and others.

We Clowns also spent some time running around the town and the island, often with me hauling bodies in the Dustmobile. I was a taxi driver without the fare and the crazy driving, but what fun! We were a tight knit faction that liked to engage in silly, fun and often questionable recreational activities.

For instance, sometimes for entertainment with friends we'd buy a bunch of bottle rockets, grab some soda bottles and take up positions across the street from each other to launch, literally, a Rocket Dodge Ball game. We'd put said rocket in a bottle, light the fuse, aim it toward the other side and let it fly at the guys across the street who were also firing rockets at us. Surprisingly, no one lost an eye or finger, but we had a ton of laughs.

We also entertained ourselves by inventing characters, human or animal.

One of the Clown-created characters that we all embraced was "The Birds," a gesture I still use today, more than 50 years later, to entertain my grandkids. It's not what you might think.

I'm not teaching the youngsters a doubly rude, middle finger salute on both hands. This one's harmless.

Back in the day, these birds took flight after one of us Clowns would lift one or both of our arms, extending them at a 90-degree angle from our body. With our arms straight out, we would begin to flap our thumbs and little fingers while maneuvering our hands through the air, making a "phoo, phoo, phoo, phoo" sound through pursed lips.

Once when I saw Hal decades after Taiwan, I launched the birds behind his back and made their noise in flight.

"Phoo, phoo, phoo, phoo."

"Arrrgggh, that sound!" he yelled.

A funny, foundational and silly memory with long-lasting power. All those years later it took Hal instantly back to 1972. One recurring problem for us when we wanted to launch a new music-inspired head trip to another dimension was finding a steady supply of marijuana. The on-base crackdown on weed importation was working and the flow had slowed. But never underestimate a resourceful American in the face of a challenge, especially one that involves getting high.

We rose to the task when we hit the bottom of a bag of weed and ran out of "shake," another of the million nicknames for leafy pot. No problem. We crunched up the remains—stems and seeds—rolled the lumpiest joint ever and fired it up. Calling the smoke and taste harsh would be an understatement.

One day we even ran out of stems and seeds. What's a head to do? One thing is to fall back on the when-in-Rome scheme. We decided to go local and try a peculiar material you could buy in the community markets.

One of the first quirky things you notice when you get to Taiwan is that many glassy-eyed people, both men and women, displayed smiles that made you stop in your tracks and say "whoa," hopefully not out loud.

That's because when they grinned you saw their teeth and gums were darkened with a foul-looking, reddish-brown stain a hundred times worse than tobacco.

These were the chewers of betel nut, the seed of the areca palm which is wrapped in a betel leaf. The concoction played an important role in Taiwan's culture and customs and is even used in some religious practices in South Asia. We really knew nothing about it other than the teeth discoloration, but we'd heard it supposedly gave you a buzz. That was enough for us. Apparently it could also cause dizziness, tremors, or diarrhea and vomiting, but we didn't bother to look too deeply into potential side effects. After you chewed it, you were supposed to either spit it out or swallow it. Sounded delightful.

We were desperate and dumb, so we bought a bag of the nuts and went to a nearby park to start the experiment. I remember being more than a little tentative, but not to be outdone I dove in and put the nut in my mouth as did my buddies.

Wow, a God-awful, sharp, bitter tang like I'd never experienced before flooded my taste buds as a powerful, pungent odor swirled up into my nose. I scrunched my cheeks up to my now-teary eyes in reaction.

I said something along the lines of, "Uggghhh," and shook my head as if I could shake out the taste. My fellow Clowns were in the throes of similar reactions. We all laughed loudly at our idiocy.

PARTNERS, CLOWNS AND BETEL JUICE

I don't remember how long we chewed, but it wasn't too long. Not one of us was brave enough to swallow the stuff. We spit the remains out in a cup. In the end, the flavor and the discomfort outweighed the slight head rush we got.

To me, a non-smoker of tobacco, it was a bit like taking a drag off a nasty cigarette and igniting a short-lived dizzying rush. That pretty much ended our do-in-Rome experiment.

25
SMUGGLING STICKS

EARLIER IN 1972 I had extended my tour in Taiwan by a year, so that meant I would stay put until February 1974 before heading home. I loved the island and the culture and Edie, of course. But somewhere along the way I began to think about how long I had been away from the states.

I arrived in Asia as an unsophisticated 18-year-old in August 1968. In the past four years I'd had only two quick, back-to-back visits to Ohio, one for my father's passing. The extension of time in Taiwan meant I'd be away from the U.S. for at least six years and would be bearing down on my mid-20s by the time I returned.

Slowly, those notions began to nag at me. How much has the World changed? How much have I changed? Well, a lot from my first days on the island, that's for sure. That span had encompassed some real coming-of-age, formative years, all of which I had spent in Asia. And being gone from my homeland for so long was starting to become a big deal to me.

But what to do about Edie? We had a serious relationship but we had not discussed marriage in the short term. As mentioned, I was still wrestling with trust issues after the scarring experience with Penny.

I know Edie would have been a great wife and despite an occasional insecure doubt, I was pretty confident she loved me.

But I began to wonder how things would work out back home if we did get married.

I hadn't been around a round-eye woman (the standard designation by GIs for American women when you were living in Asia) for years. Would I regret bringing Edie home? My Catholicism wormed its way into my thinking. I wondered if I would have the moral strength to remain faithful to her when surrounded by the temptation of American girls who I had only minimal experience with, at best. Instinctively I knew, based on my initial sexual escapade with a woman the first time I went to downtown Taichung, the answer was pretty obvious.

In honesty, I realized that being true might be a shaky proposition at best. I kicked these deliberations around for a while and ultimately decided to pull the plug on my year's extension. With mixed emotions, I made the decision to cancel that extra time and go back home in several months in February 1973.

Sharing the news with Edie was certainly a difficult and painful conversation. It had to be because apparently I've blacked it out. Try as I might, I'm unable to bring up one particular scene in memory where I dropped that particular bomb that I was leaving earlier than she expected.

Even thinking about it now creates a stitch in my gut, an empty feeling. I know I made noises to her about still finding a way to make our relationship continue after I left. It's doubtful that either one of us believed that malarkey. I was torn because I knew how wonderful a human being she was.

At times I've wondered where she might be all these years later. Did she find another American boyfriend and end up back here after all? Wherever she ended up, I hope she has a brood of kids because she had a special affinity for children.

Many years ago I made a half-hearted attempt to track her down through one of my former Chinese police partners, but I gave it up too easily after some initial inquiries. In the long run, of course, leaving was the right decision. If nothing else, the fact that my instincts told me I might stray once we got to the U.S. suggests my love might not have run as deep as I thought it did at the time.

Certainly, I saved her future heartache and the wasted time she would have spent relocating halfway across the world with a knucklehead with iffy-at-times moral convictions.

Over those nearly five years in Southeast Asia I'd had so many amazing experiences and seen so many unique things in a world that had been alien to me in the beginning. I'd traveled roads, most legal, some not, that I would never have gone down had I not come to Taiwan.

It was only later I realized that many of my activities and behaviors shared a common underpinning—my love for the adrenalin and stream of energy sparked by new adventures.

Heading back home was certainly going to open another door to new escapades and it was something to look forward to. But, of course, me being me, it was not quite enough.

I had to ratchet up the thrills by contriving a risky, crazy and, yes, brainless plot to bring a little something back from Asia because my stereo system, rattan papa-san and mama-san chairs, wood carvings and tailor-made suits were not enough.

My buddy Trash Can had been reassigned to Korat Air Base in northeast Thailand and I had enough leave time accumulated for a quick visit there before I left for home. I liked Trash and looked forward to seeing him, but my trip was cover for the real mission—to purchase easily obtainable Thai sticks and smuggle them back first to Taiwan and then to the states.

See what I mean? Risky and dumb. An American caught in a foreign land smuggling illegal drugs meant certain jail time, especially in those days. And what I would find behind those prison walls should I get caught would be the direct opposite of a country club-style jailhouse. I knew it was dodgy but I was confident I could pull it off.

In the dominion of weed with kick-ass impact, Thai sticks resided at the top of the stoner's pyramid. They were a sought-after commodity. Typically, the sticks were made from the cured flower of a marijuana plant, skewered on a bamboo stick and wrapped and tied together with hemp string.

At times, they might even be dipped in opium. Yep, that weed was robust, alright. The sticks varied in length, but the ones I saw were typically about six inches long. A "brick" of Thai sticks would consist of about 20-to-22 sticks.

About a month before I left for the World, I flew to the city of Bangkok, Thailand's capital. This congested city is known as the Venice of the East because of the muddy brown Chao Phraya River and several canals that flow through it.

Making Taichung almost seem rural in comparison, traffic gridlocks clogged Bangkok's streets with cars, buses, motorcycles and pedicabs. Toss in the river and canals, which were also hectic thoroughfares and were like Bangkok's highways without asphalt, and nuttiness was guaranteed.

Sightseeing boats, river buses and long water boat taxis competed for space with families floating along in tiny dinghies.

Crisscrossing wakes rippled across the muddy water as vessels angled for position while passing slower-moving craft.

Vendors hawked fruit, vegetables and mystery meat from stands stretching along the banks. Half-dressed kids splashed and frolicked in the opaque liquid flowing by, containing who knows what assortment of waste and pollutants.

Once I checked into my hotel I hit the streets in mission-primed mode, ready to take the first step in the operation. It took less than an hour.

"Hey GI, you look for something?" said one young Thai man, sidling up as I sat on the side of a small fountain, quietly scoping out the scene while trying to figure out how to make something happen.

"Yeah, I might be. What are you talking about?"

I was more than a little nervous. Was this a set up? Was this guy a cop out to entrap and arrest me right after I bought an illegal substance?

"What you want GI? You want boom-boom? I find you pretty girl. She wait for you."

"No, man, not looking for any boom-boom. Is that all you're selling?"

"No, what you want? What you look for?

I hesitated to say it out loud, but no ask, no score. I could always claim I didn't understand his English or his meaning if it turned out this guy was an undercover cop. I tried coy, or at least what I thought passed for coy.

"You have smoke? I'm looking for smoke." Hey, I might mean cigarettes, OK.

"Ah," he said with a laugh. "Sure GI, you looky for grass. You want Thai stick?"

"Yes, Thai stick, that's what I want."

So much for being coy and cunning.

"OK, you wait here. I be back."

He walked away and I envisioned him coming back leading a platoon of uniformed police officers. But a few minutes later he returned with a bicycle loaded down with canvas bags. He opened one sack and turned it toward me. Inside I saw stacks of bricks of Thai sticks. Another smaller bag held individually wrapped grams of hashish.

"How much you want?" he asked.

"Uh, how much is it?"

As it turned out, it wasn't really that much. I'm pretty sure I didn't even try to haggle with the guy because it was so cheap. I walked away with three bricks of Thai stick—more than 60 sticks in all—and a few grams of hash for $6. Yep, $6, American.

I wasted no time going back up to the room to, you know, test the product. It tested well. So well, in fact, I spent most of my time in Bangkok and in Korat in a pleasant haze.

Once again, not my proudest moment but if you turn a kid loose in a candy store, well, you know, they consume a lot of candy. This was more proof that while I had added years to my existence since coming to Asia, the wisdom side of me was still struggling and failing to keep up.

I spent little time soaking up the local culture and beauty of a unique country. Nonetheless, the first leg of my mission was accomplished. I had the product.

Now, could I get it back to Taiwan without getting caught and tossed in prison for like forever? Failing would be the ultimate life-changing bummer. But the adrenaline was certainly amped high.

SMUGGLING STICKS

One problem I realized early on was that I bought way more weed than I could smuggle back. I smoked a lot and even loaded up a couple of peanut butter sandwiches with grass for lunch. And I still had a large quantity of reefer remaining.

Before I left for Taiwan, I flushed great gobs of it down the toilet, praying I wouldn't clog the pipes. I couldn't put the dope in my suitcase, of course. Pot-sniffing dogs patrolled airports everywhere, especially when travelers were leaving out of a dope mecca like Thailand.

But I had formulated an idea which I thought was pretty ingenious—bring the stuff back in my military hat, which would sit on top of my head and (hopefully) out of range from any nosy mutts. I might have reconsidered this genius of an idea had I bothered to research just how powerful a dog's nose is. Their snouts have 100s of millions of olfactory receptors and their sense of smell is hundreds to thousands of times stronger than ours. Like I said, my wisdom development was lagging far behind my chronological development.

So I proceeded. A military service cap is round in form with a crown and a short, gloss black visor in front. A circular fiber and wire grommet creates and holds the circle's form at the top of the hat.

I had the bright idea to replace the standard grommet with a thick, hollow rubber tube. I could stuff the weed inside the tube, circle it and close it, insert it into my service cap and presto, just another serviceman heading through an airport.

At least, that was my hope.

Hanging on to my best poker face when I got to Bangkok's airport, I approached customs as my stomach liberated a battalion of butterflies and I tried not to think about sweating. But no one asked me to remove my hat and I passed through the checkpoints without a hitch. Nonetheless, smuggling illegal substances atop your head is hair raising (pun intended) and rough on the nerves. Did I mention it was over-the-top illegal? I wouldn't recommend trying it.

But I got back to CCK without incident. I didn't have much time left on the island by then. I knew when I returned to the states, I'd have to gear up my courage to face the gauntlet of customs once again.

Despite knowing this was an immense and ill-advised risk, the reward overshadowed my worry of potential danger. I just didn't think too much about it and I was confident I'd get through it all. And just before I was set to depart the island, the military threw me an interesting and unexpected curve ball.

But first, I had to plow through my final days on Town Patrol as I tried to wrap my mind around the chores of packing up and leaving Edie and returning to America.

Beginning barely out of my childhood and teen years, I'd been a cop for nearly five years, survived bar fights, racial confrontations, typhoons, rocket attacks in Vietnam, friends suffering heroin withdrawals and a cheating fiancée. I'd made many close friends and fallen in love a second time with a beautiful woman who I was now going to leave behind.

My emotions roiled as I prepared for departure. Ironically, even the ground shook a little before I left. One early morning Edie and I were awakened to the sight of our overhead ceiling light swaying back and forth as the earth rippled with tremors. It seemed to last four and a half hours, but in reality it was short. Nonetheless, that's a wake-up call when you are on the third floor!

I was torn about my looming return home. When I first came to Taiwan, I had been homesick for about six months. Guys who had been here, went home and then came back—and many did—warned me that when I got back to the states I would find myself homesick for Taiwan.

I scoffed at that notion, but soon enough I would discover how correct they were. Once back home and for about a half year, I longed for the culture, the people—Edie especially—and the beauty of Taiwan.

I finished my duty with TAFP on February 10, 1973 and once again, much like I experienced many years before in Columbus, I felt like I was saying goodbye to my family. What a great run in a unique and extraordinary unit. I was luckier than most of the cops who never got to work downtown or at best often served less than a year on Town Patrol. Though the time was split, I had been in the unit for nearly two years.

During my last week and with only a few days left before shipping out, the Air Force dropped a bombshell on me. I was ordered to escort a prisoner back to Lowry Air Force Base in Colorado when I left Taiwan. Wow, man!

Talk about irony: a cop with a hat full of dope escorting a prisoner back to the states. You can't make up this kind of stuff, and I'm not now.

As strange as the circumstances were, I realized I had just been handed a modicum of cover. It seemed highly unlikely anyone would suspect me of being involved in an illegal smuggling activity with a prisoner on my arm.

Finally the time came to say goodbye to Edie. It was rough. After a fitful night of little sleep, we got up before dawn so I could catch my ride to CCK. I remember standing in the small dimly lit courtyard outside of our apartment while it was still cool and dark out and wet from an overnight rain.

Once again I was saying goodbye to a loved one with tears and promises and hugs and kisses. With an ache in my heart, I looked back at her as I walked out of the front gate for the last time. I had resolved to stay in contact after I was settled in at my next assignment, Hamilton Air Force Base in the San Francisco Bay Area, which ironically was my Clown buddy Red's hometown. Somewhere inside I clung tentatively to a belief that Edie and I might still work things out, but I had to put my feet on American soil first.

I never saw her again. I wrote letters and a couple were answered but then we stopped. Another important early-in-life love affair evaporated. Had I stayed longer and not canceled my extension of time in Taiwan, it's likely we would have gotten married. How different my life would have turned out had that happened. Who knows, perhaps I'd be living on the island even now like some of my friends still do. But it wasn't meant to be.

The prisoner I escorted back to the states had committed a crime, but it was not so momentous that I can recall now what he had done. I wasn't armed, he wasn't dangerous and I remember he was friendly enough that we shared stories on the flight back home. In short, he was an excellent travel companion and perfect cover for my own law-breaking behavior. Again, not one of my finest moments.

Talk about double standards. We saw one drug dog in the airport in Taipei but he never got close to the two of us. And of course I didn't tell my companion that I was lugging extra illicit baggage.

SMUGGLING STICKS

I dropped the guy off at Lowry without incident and made my way to Columbus. Once back home, I was the man of the hour for many of my pot-smoking friends who had heard about, but never smoked, Thai sticks.

They found the smuggling tale entertaining and I don't regret I did it, but man, the consequences had I been caught would have been tragic for my future and my freedom! Totally crazy, a phrase I've heard more than once when someone has suggested that might be the proper meaning of my adopted initials, TC.

EPILOGUE

I STARTED THIS NARRATIVE pointing out how young and dumb I was when I first left Ohio for Asia. Over the ensuing years, the young slowly worked its way out. But clearly my parting act as I left Taiwan revealed I was still clinging tightly to the dumb.

When I left home, I was clueless to how the world really worked and how different life and living were in dissimilar parts of the planet. At 18, I was confident that the person I was then was who I would be for the rest of my life. I hadn't yet grasped how much growing up still lay ahead. Certainly I was influenced by the radical '60s and '70s and all the societal upheaval that came with those explosive times.

Being so youthful, I didn't really grasp with any depth what I was doing half the time. More often, I simply chose not to delve too deeply into my activities and how they might impact or influence people or situations around me. And like many from my generation, I resisted authority figures, ironically ignoring the fact that as a cop I, too, represented authority.

Like many of us Baby Boomers, I wanted to change the world and make it a better place. For sure, I changed my own personal world and developed a persona with both good and bad characteristics. Living during a tumultuous period in a culture completely alien to everything I had previously known or experienced brought transformations I never imagined when I left the states.

Along the way and after nearly five years in East and Southeast Asia, I had absorbed and adopted many of the lessons that those times and places offered. I had survived countless potential hazardous situations, sometimes just barely. Some were unexpected or related to the kind of circumstances that I found myself in as a police officer. Some I brought upon myself by my own careless actions, including that near life-ending tumble down an extended flight of stairs.

By the time I turned 23, I was not even close to the person I had been as a child and teenager. In those early days. I had no clue about the outlandish and deep experiences that lie ahead of me or the range of influential personalities that would cross my path when I first arrived in Asia.

I was no longer a green kid; I was harder and clearly a hypocrite in some of the ways I chose to live. In truth, I was no different than many other people: I had discovered that I had a dark side that I could and would engage when it was beneficial to me.

But there was quality growth, too. I had learned to love the Chinese people and their society. While they too can cling to ego and power and greed, so many of their customs were fascinating, different and embraceable. Though not all of the locals were big fans of Americans, many were.

Universally, the people of Taiwan were kind and caring. While their customs were strange to me at first, I eventually grew to appreciate many of their cultural touchstones, including family loyalty, reverence for elders, a robust ambition for work and education and a conscious effort to avoid embarrassing others by making them "lose face."

EPILOGUE

I still mentally kick myself for not making a major effort to learn the Mandarin language while I was there, as some of the smarter guys like Danny Lever had done. Had I done so I would have greatly enriched my appreciation for the culture and it likely would have changed my life in completely different and unpredictable ways.

Although I hadn't bothered to take a deep dive into their lingo, by the time I left I could understand the gist of conversations between people thanks to all of my work with local Chinese police and the people of Taichung who we interacted with daily. To this day I still recognize that language when I hear it on the street.

My initial homesickness had disappeared after my first six months on the island and I started to feel comfortable and at home. Surprisingly, I even began to enjoy the duties of being a cop. When the Air Force officially made that my first career, I was as shocked about that selection as everyone who knew me was! My life up to that point had been about avoiding confrontations.

In Taiwan, I was tossed in the middle of conflicts and bar fights on a regular basis. Every day was exciting and challenging and different from the previous day. Admittedly after doing the job for a while, I grew disenchanted with people in general. As a cop you run into more assholes than good guys.

No doubt those countless stressful encounters taught me to react more with anger, defensiveness and pessimism to life's little obstacles. Those persistent clashes didn't totally erase hope and caring from my psyche, but I became more realistic, at least I thought, in my assessment of people and life's events. Smooth sailing was never guaranteed and life's conditions could toss you around when you least expected it. But as we said back in the day, it was always better if you could go with the flow, difficult as that might be. Or adopt this attitude: "It don't mean nothin'!"

But my experiences weren't all horrible and a whole lot of it was fun.

The Taichung Armed Forces Police unit was exceptional at that time and I was extremely lucky to be a part of it. A few years after I left the island, Town Patrol was diminished and eventually disbanded as American troops slowly withdrew from Taiwan in the wake of President Richard Nixon opening diplomatic relations with China in early 1972. I haven't been back to the island since I left in February 1973, but from images and reports from friends who still live there, I would no longer recognize the place. It's a far cry from the Third World backwater it once was. Taichung, the second largest city and the island's arts and cultural center, is a booming metropolis, populated with numerous high-rise buildings. The population grew from 400,000 when I was there to nearly 1.8 million people today.

But I was in Taichung and CCK at the height and excitement of it all—the close camaraderie with the other guys, the stand-out uniform with a badge and cool arm band, and the every-night exhilaration of helping people in trouble, enforcing the law, pushing troublemakers into the van's cage and protecting my partners' backs.

It could be hard and sometimes dangerous work, but I discovered I was able to overcome fear and sum up the courage and heart to do what was needed. It was almost like my real-life version of those childhood fantasies of being Spiderman, swinging into action!

EPILOGUE

There were other perils, too. I had experienced first-hand the evil of war—a wasteful expenditure of young lives. Our mistaken involvement in the Vietnam conflict left me and many of my military brethren embittered. And you could get killed.

Adding insult to that jumble of emotions was the absence of any "welcome home" when we Vietnam vets came back. We weren't seen as patriots who served our country. Instead we were villains and killers in the eyes of many American civilians, who also hated the war. I don't think any of us expected parades, but we also didn't anticipate being shunned, either.

Over time I had learned the value of close relationships. I had discovered what it was like to fall in love and set up a household and live with a partner. And I found the trauma that love could also bring along with its companions, heartbreak and anger. Living through all of that distress exposed an unexpected dark side of myself that was unsettling and troublesome.

No matter how good I thought I was, I was capable of crossing lines and even hurting other people to get what I wanted or to exact revenge. In other words, people can't always be trusted, including myself. Or put another way, "I'm an ass, you're an ass."

For sure I had discovered a previously dormant, inner crazy streak after I was turned loose in Asia. In no time, I let my freak flag fly and I enjoyed the hell out of it. For a time I resisted getting pulled into this stream of foolishness, but once my toes hit those waters it became easier to do stupid and sketchy things.

Examining this time of my life after so many years was a lot to absorb, and it was sobering and educational. Besides reliving many of these experiences, I achieved another benefit from this project. With some persistent effort, I was able to track down about a dozen former friends and partners more than five decades after last seeing them.

Some I called and others I reunited with in person, including my Clown brothers Rick Campbell and Hal Thoms, work buddy Ulysses Bryant and patrol and party partner Al Hoover, who gave me my life-long nickname. When Al and I first talked on the phone after so many decades, he had trouble remembering me, which is absolutely hilarious and filled with irony since that nickname changed my life.

Even though I had some nervous reservations about reconnecting with these guys, every one of them was happy that I had reached across the years to find them. Gerody "Boat" Boatwright told me: "You're the only one I've ever talked to from Taiwan days."

Not surprising and sadly, I also discovered that some of these close friends, like my former mentor Harry Eaton and Kentucky wild man Tom Collins, were now gone. Other deceased close associates and partners include "Jumpin' Joe Blaise—jokingly named for his deliberate responses to most things—and John Porter, who swore I would weigh 300 pounds when I got older. Sorry John, I do not, nor have I ever, approached that number.

Each time I learned the unwelcome news that a friend had passed was a kick in the gut and it just made me wish I had started this search years ago. Other guys I wanted to find, like Isaac Chavez and Ray Hernandez, eluded my searches.

But the more I thought about all the people I grew close to in Taiwan, the more it became clear to me that working with, and especially having fun and carousing with, these guys played an overpowering role in my life. They were my brothers—partners for life, as Ulysses likes to say today.

EPILOGUE

I also grew to understand how I used entertainment as a way to connect with people, cover up a niggling shyness and escape from the crappy things that never ceased to pop up in life, especially in military life.

I wanted to be liked and respected and I wanted to gain confidence and self-esteem. I believe I did achieve all of that, but way too often the vehicle I chose to get there was partying.

That festive way of life became a driving force in my formative years and it hasn't completely vanished, though the passage of time has had a definite impact and has helped slow my roll on all the wildness. Mulling it over, I think my actions often reflected my desire from childhood to live out that Peter-Pan lifestyle of never growing up.

In the end, everything in those years—the good times, the menacing times, the miserable times, the foolish fun times and the eye-opening awakening to new and unique cultures—shaped who I would become and who I am now. And good or bad, that person is not remotely like the unaware 18-year-old who left home for adventure on a dreary March morning in 1968. I came out on the other side with a new name, an attitude inclined to pleasurable experiences and an understanding that my ambition to help others is shaded by my own dark side.

In other words, I was made in Taiwan.

PHOTOS

Graduation picture from Security Police Tech School, Lackland Air Force Base, Texas.

Typical traffic in Taipei, Taiwan.

All dresed up to guard aircraft at CCK Airbase in Taichung.

Game on with my M-16 on the CCK flightline.

PHOTOS

My CCK buddies enjoying our favorite after-work activity.

Pre-shift TAFP guardmount inspection.

A typical end-of-shift party with my Town Patrol partners in the Hostel, including Alvin Hoover (R sitting), who nicknamed me TCB in 1969, and Danny Lever standing behind him.

With my partner Ulysses Bryant outside of TAFP HQ.

PHOTOS

My workplace - The Dirty Dozen.

Partners Lewis Waters (L) and Ulysses Bryant (R) kicking back at the USO with a buddy downtown.

Penny and me struggling to stay upright.

Me and my dad Ed in our last picture in 1969 before I left for Vietnam.

PHOTOS

My hootch at Bien Hoa Airbase, Vietnam.

Watchtower at Bien Hoa Airbase, Vietnam.

MADE IN TAIWAN

Hard at work in underground tactical operations center in Vietnam.

Down time at Bien Hoa Airbase, Vietnam.

PHOTOS

Vietnamese band entertains the troops at Bien Hoa Airbase, Vietnam.

Nightly entertainment in Vietnam - Beer Can Jenga.

"Country Willie" holds court in our hootch at Bien Hoa, Vietnam.

"Country Willie" belting out a tune in our hootch at Bien Hoa, Vietnam.

PHOTOS

Temple in Taipei, Taiwan, the island's capital.

Colorful dragon in Taichung parade.

Edie and me taking a breather after a tough walk in front of an also breath-taking background.

Edie adding beauty to a beautiful garden.

PHOTOS

Girlfriend Edie flashes the popular sign of the times.

The Dustmobile, always primed to explore.

MADE IN TAIWAN

The Clowns, Hal Thoms and Rick Campbell, boarding the Dustmobile.

Dave Kinney (floor), Hal Thoms (visor) and Rick Campbell, aka Clowns, kick back in my Taichung apartment.

PHOTOS

Making a public statement outside of the barracks at CCK Airbase, Taiwan.

In 2022, 53 years after Al Hoover nicknamed me TC, we reunited in Topsail, N.C.

In 2023, Ulysses Bryant and I recreated a pose we first did in front of the TAFP HQ building 54 years ago.

The Clowns, minus one, reunite in Vegas in 2023 for more mischief, 52 years after our first capers. Rick Campbell (l), me and Hal Thoms.

ACKNOWLEDGEMENTS

OFTEN ONE PERSON WRITES a book, but the author's efforts are buoyed by a supporting cast who are invisible in the wings. My supporting cast was especially strong, starting with my loving wife, Mary Yost, a stellar former journalist and editor who encouraged me in the dark moments over two years when I was ready to trash this project. She kept me on track. Death claimed Mary's light before this memoir could get published, but she read and edited the book twice and she made it sparkle. Without her, this may never have seen the light of day. You truly were the "clean up woman" Mary, and my gratitude to you rests forever in my heart, as do you.

Part of my research required me to track down guys I served with in Asia who I had last spoken with more than 50 years ago, in the late 1960s or early 1970s. While I zeroed in on a dozen or more people, I was fortunate to find Alvin Hoover, who bequeathed me with the nickname "TC" in 1969. Without a doubt, that changed my life to some extent. But the most hilarious thing happened after I reached him these many years later and he told me he did not remember me. You got to love irony. Al and I spent time catching up, on the phone and in person, and reminiscing about long ago, which added detail to my story. Thank you so much for all you did, Al.

Another must-find for me was Ulysses Bryant, my man who was a great partner to have by your side in a bar scuffle. Uly is a big guy who came to us from the Boston Armed Forces Police, so advantage to me in those dust ups. We talked many times on the phone and met up for dinner in Savannah, reviewing my photo albums from way back then and telling a few tales. Uly, thank you so much for all the friendship, backup and caring. As you have said, "partners forever."

I found several other former Town Patrol members who played a critical role to help me fill in some of the blank spots or questionable memories. Those friends include Danny Lever, Jarema "Myk" Mykitschak, Lewis Waters, David "Trashcan" Worthen, Gerody "Boat" Boatwright, Hal Thoms and former Chinese MP Sean Shih. I can't thank you guys enough for your willingness to talk and remember with me. Promise I'll send y'all a book!

And where would this work be without Beta readers? I recruited some good ones who proffered insightful advice. First readers included one of the OC's - original "Clowns" - Rick Campbell, who I've never lost connection with. Other readers were: Rick Mountain, best-name-ever for a book or movie character, who was also stationed in Taiwan and who still lives there, my cousin Fred Zicard, former newspaper colleague and author Jack Torry, Washington D.C. book agent Diane Nine and, of course, my wife and editor Mary.

My apologies if I failed to mention someone. In truth, every personal connection I made way back in those long-ago days was instrumental in getting me to the here and now. Many thanks and much love to all.

T.C. BROWN is a former newspaper journalist for multiple publications in California, Ohio and Kentucky, including the *Plain Dealer* of Cleveland, *The Columbus Dispatch* and the *Kentucky Post*. His investigative work led to an appearance on ABC-TV's *Nightline*. He has been a free-lance writer for local, state and national publications, including the *New York Times*, *Columbia Journalism Review* and *Playboy* magazine. He was a Kiplinger Digital Media Fellow at The Ohio State University and has been a long-time communication consultant, including running the national Twitter feed for a grassroots, pro-democracy group. He was an adjunct professor of journalism at Ohio Wesleyan University. National, state and local organizations have awarded his work, including the National Press Club, the National Association of Capitol Reporters and Editors and Ohio Society of Professional Journalists, among others. From 1968 to 1973 he was an Air Force military policeman in Taiwan and Vietnam. He lives in Columbus, Ohio, and this recounting of his time in Asia is his first book.

www.ingramcontent.com/pod-product-compliance
Lightning Source LLC
Chambersburg PA
CBHW030534080526
44586CB00011B/438